Krysia,

Always Keep The
Faith!
(Especially In "The Landing!")

Mike Mulhern

Bring the Rain

A True Story of Healing and Heaven

Mike Mitchener

(With blog entries
by Victoria Mitchener Power)

WESTBOW
PRESS®
A DIVISION OF THOMAS NELSON
& ZONDERVAN

WestBow Press books may be ordered through booksellers or by contacting:

WestBow Press
A Division of Thomas Nelson & Zondervan
1663 Liberty Drive
Bloomington, IN 47403
www.westbowpress.com
1 (866) 928-1240

ISBN: 978-1-5127-6088-0 (sc)
ISBN: 978-1-5127-6329-4 (hc)
ISBN: 978-1-5127-6087-3 (e)

Library of Congress Control Number: 2016917398

Print information available on the last page.

WestBow Press rev. date: 12/2/2016

Foreword

On the morning of September 12, 2014, at roughly 5:45 a.m., I received the following text message: "Mike had a massive heart attack. He is in critical condition." Typically I'm not awake at such an early hour; however, for some reason I was on this day. I immediately called the person who sent the text, and all he knew was that our dear friend was fighting for his life. I packed a bag and headed for Daytona Beach. The drive from Tampa was difficult for me. My own father had died one month earlier, and I missed seeing him alive by fourteen hours. In my mind, I was once again racing against the inevitable. I wanted to see Mike before he passed.

Everyone has a Mike Mitchener story. Mine dates back almost twenty years. I was sixteen years old and a cart pusher for the Sarasota Sam's Club. Mike was the general manager. Our paths rarely crossed at work, yet Mike had the unique ability to make anyone feel special, particularly those who worked for him. Eight years later, I was an assistant manager at the Daytona Beach Sam's Club. The announcement was made that Mike Mitchener would become our new general manager.

During those days, Mike tried to break me. No matter what happened, it was my fault. It was clear to me that Mike was an extraordinary leader but also very difficult to please! I didn't realize it at the time, but this was his plan from the beginning. He pushed me beyond my capacity at times. Secretly he would tell others, "This kid is special, and I'll be working for him someday." Mike was really good to me. For over two years he invested much of his time and energy in me, and to this day I've not had another career mentor like him. I am where I am today largely because of Mike. Aside from work, Mike also became a close friend. Someone once told me that in life one only has about five true friends. Mike is certainly one of my five!

Racing against the clock, my mind was full of thoughts. How? Why? What if? In between thoughts were the phone calls. I began to connect the dots as information came in, and this tragic story started to become even more real. Sometime around eight thirty in the morning, I entered Halifax Hospital. I walked into Mike's hospital room, and there he was—almost unrecognizable among the tubes and machines. I sat next to him and began studying the equipment: each machine, monitor, tube, alarm, and the many wires. *This can't be,* I thought. I touched his arm, and he felt abnormally cold. For two hours I sat by his side, listening to the nurses, doctors, and specialists discuss his case. I learned they lowered his body temperature intentionally to slow his brain activity. I became obsessed with finding out everything I could about Mike's condition. I believe it was therapeutic for me to know and understand the details. It kept my mind off the constant worry that he would die. While his friends and family were making their journeys to see Mike, I was able to spend a few hours alone with my friend. Not knowing if he could hear me, I spoke to him as if he could. I laughed and cried and prayed. There were moments of extreme silence. All I could think of was, *Why him?*

Later that afternoon, I greeted several of Mike's family members and friends as they arrived. I filled them in with the details and watched them run through their own processes of understanding what was happening. The support was amazing. Mike received hundreds of visitors. In fact, Halifax Hospital had to rewrite its visitor/guest policy based on the number of people who came to see Mike. Social media and the Internet played a huge role. Mike's oldest child, Victoria, sent out multiple daily updates on a web page dedicated to his progress. When it was all said and done, Mike's web site page had over twenty thousand hits! Everyone stepped up to help out. Our friend Joe Dunlop even mowed Mike's grass. For those of you who know Mike, clearly he is too cheap to invest in a riding lawn mower, so Joe pushed through eight-inch-tall St. Augustine grass row by row!

As you will read, the hours turned into days, and each of us waited anxiously for Mike to wake up. That day eventually came, and I was able to be there with him. After they removed the breathing tube, Mike was able to speak. I remember telling him he sounded like Batman. He laughed. He was back. My friend was back. Statistically Mike should not be with us today. I don't know why God allowed him to come back to us. Perhaps it is you. Mike has an amazing impact on others. It is my belief that God wants Mike's story to be known so that others might choose to follow him. My hope is that this story will touch each of its readers in a special way. Since the event, Mike has had the opportunity to tell his story to countless individuals. In the pages ahead, you will learn why so many of us love him. From his hometown beginnings to his professional baseball career, we can all identify with something in his story. To me, the story isn't just about a man who died and went to heaven. It is a story about the American dream. Mike demonstrates that with faith, family, and a little work ethic anything is possible. The story also points out that life is like a vapor; we are only here for a moment.

—Darrell Arnold

From the Author

This book was written for those of you who have faith in God but have never had the opportunity to experience the value of that faith. The number of people in my life who have helped me understand the value of faith are too many to list here. Please know that I carry each one of you in my heart. I hope this book will inspire and encourage you to keep believing.

—Mike

Prologue

Everything is going dark.

I'm alone.

Where am I?

"Bring me joy ..."

I'm on my knees, looking down at the pavement.

Why?

What happened?

"Bring me peace ..."

I don't remember.

I can't get up.

Everything feels so heavy.

"Bring the chance to be free ..."

What happened?

This weight on my chest is too much.

Where am I? Oh, that's right, the gym. I'm in the parking lot next to my truck.

"Bring me anything that brings you glory ..."

Why can't I stand up?

My legs don't work.

Why does my whole body feel so heavy?

"And I know there'll be days ..."

What should I do?

I can't even yell for help.

I'm too far from the door or the rest of the people inside.

"When this life brings me pain ..."

My chest really hurts!

I was at the gym!

I was at work just an hour ago!

What happened?

"But if that's what it takes to praise you ..."

I'm alone.

Am I dying?

I'm going to die in this parking lot ... alone.

But I wasn't alone.

I was never alone.

"Jesus, bring the rain."

Introduction

It was a normal day for me, completely normal. I did the usual things of waking up, getting ready to go to work at Sam's Club, checking in with associates, reviewing the store to prepare for opening, logging on to the computer, checking yesterday's numbers, and reviewing plans for today. Normal. Absolutely and completely normal.

Eleven. That number has always carried significant meaning to me. For as long as I can remember, it always just stood out to me, whether I was looking at a digital alarm or wall clock that read 11:11 or being assigned a number for a team jersey. That number just seemed to appear. Consequently, eleven became my favorite number. Like many people, September eleventh has carried special meaning for many years. As a matter of fact, I have always considered eleven to be somewhat lucky for me. I'm not sure why, but the number eleven just always seemed to "show up."

It was September 11, 2014. On that day, as well as the other anniversaries of that tragedy, I woke up to the thought of the innocent people who died on the planes that crashed in New York City, Washington, DC, and Pennsylvania. I thought about them meeting God and seeing heaven and loved ones who were taken to heaven before them. I absolutely didn't think about anything bad happening to me. Come on now, I am six feet three inches tall and weigh 240 pounds, and I work out all the time. As a matter of fact, in twenty-four years with Sam's Club, I have never missed a day of work or taken a sick day. I'm only forty-seven years old. I go to the gym to take care of my body. Our bodies are gifts, and I've always wanted to preserve that gift and take care of myself. As a matter of fact, I had been doing so for almost twenty years. I am not a gym nut, but I know the value of working out. It builds up your strength reserve. It clears your mind. It keeps you healthy.

I left work at 5:30 p.m. on Thursday, September 11, 2014. I went to the gym and trained. I grabbed my stuff, and I walked out the door. Unbeknownst to me, not only was I walking out of the gym but I was walking out of my old life and into my new life.

This is my story.

CHAPTER 1

Early Years

My town did not have a hospital, so my Mom and Dad headed over to Marion to bring me into the world. It was October 2, 1966. My hometown is actually Gas City, Indiana, which is roughly five miles south of Marion. My mother and father are wonderful people. They were married in early 1966, and they both understood the value of a hard day's work and a good upbringing. Even though they were young themselves, they knew how to raise a child the right way. My father was twenty-one when I was born, and my mother was nineteen. Needless to say, they had their work cut out for them.

Living in Gas City, the value of work was a priority. Our town had two major glass factories that served as the primary places of employment. My dad's mother and stepfather worked at one of the factories. My father decided that he didn't want to work in that same factory. He wanted more. My dad wanted to be an attorney. He had worked hard at getting good grades and developing study habits to achieve this goal. My parents met at Murray State University in Murray, Kentucky. My mother was extremely intelligent, and like my father, she wanted a college degree. But once they were married, things changed.

After I was born, my mother and father started on their quest to provide a better life for their family. It was not easy. A day in the life of a young couple in Gas City with a new baby looked a little like this: Dad and Mom woke up and got ready for the day. Mom went off to work. Dad watched me. Mom came home from work, and I would be "expressing myself" in my crib while Dad would be asleep on the couch! It's easy now to see why in retrospect—as I am a father myself. Once when Dad was taking care of me, I was riding my tricycle in the house. Despite my dad's warnings about my speed, I was doing my best A.J. Foyt imitation. Even at age three, I was aware that we were living in the Indianapolis 500 state. Before too long, I crashed. My forehead above my right eye came into contact with the coffee table, and blood was everywhere. My dad, who was not a big fan of blood, remained calm but was understandably shaken. He scooped me up onto his shoulder and prepared to get me to the hospital. He had me hold a towel to my head. He wasn't sure how bad the gash was and certainly wasn't going to waste time trying to find out. As he rounded the corner past the kitchen, I stopped him. With one hand holding the towel to my bloody face, I pointed to the top of the refrigerator with my free hand. I was pointing to the now visible bananas on top of the fridge, saying, "Dad, can I have a banana before we go?" My dad remembers thinking with relief, *What a tough kid!* I got about seven stitches, and my scar has since faded. My memories of those days with my dad will stay with me forever.

There is no more important job in the world than that of a parent. My parents did not have it easy, but they understood their responsibilities and values. They passed important skills to both of their children. Once Mom got home from work, Dad would get ready for school. He had to travel about forty miles to attend Ball State University. He told me a number of times that he wanted to go to law school, but being a father was much more important. As Dad continued with his education, Mom would watch me after working all day. She would continue caring for me and get me ready for bed. Dad would come home from school tired. He would see Mom for a few hours, and she too was tired. They would spend some time together, and then my dad would be off to work at the factory from eleven in the evening until seven in the morning. This routine would go on for four years until my sister was born.

My mom told me that our family didn't have much money during these times. We had love, trust, loyalty, and compassion. Those things don't cost anything, but they carry immeasurable worth. Dinner was usually navy beans. However, my mom worked her magic in the kitchen and made those beans into magnificent varieties. One night it was navy beans and cornbread. Yummy! The next night it was navy beans and onions. Sweet! Other nights she might introduce some bacon in there, and that was special! The lesson I learned from these times (and I have just recently begun to understand it in my current role) was that it wasn't about what we had to eat. Rather, it was about the fact that we ate it together. I learned early the treasures of family bonds.

Eating dinner together is such a lost art in today's society.

Turn the cell phones off, put them away, and eat together. Talk about life—good and bad. Laugh together. Get mad together. Learn to lean on your family in good and bad times. You never really know when you might need them; funny how that seems to apply to me more realistically now.

My sister, Kim, came along in October of 1970. I was the stereotypical big brother, wishing to protect her. No one was going to hurt my sister. When she was born, my father had already graduated from Ball State. It was a milestone, as he was the only one from his family to graduate from college. He had taken a job with State Farm Insurance and was making his way. Mom decided to stop working and take care of her family full time. Our family was growing, and it was time to "move up."

CHAPTER 2

Learning Faith

Sometime in the early 1970s we moved into a different house just a few blocks from our first home. We were the typical American family. Dad worked Monday through Friday. We attended church on Sunday. Faith—this is a word that carries deeper meanings to those who have it. Faith can also apply to so many different situations in one's life. For me, faith means belief. Faith is what one believes in. I have been asked several times about my faith. I don't answer right away. I wait for that proverbial second question. Sometimes it comes as a question: "What do you believe in?" Once again I wait. I do this because I believe in many things. I believe all people are inherently good. Yes, on the surface some folks appear to be unlike me in terms of what they stand for, who they associate with, and which principles they live by. But I look at all people from the inside out. All of us bleed red. All of us have hearts that beat in similar fashion. As we move outward, the differences become more apparent.

As Christians, our actions flow from our sense of gratitude

for the gift of salvation we have been given. We haven't done anything to earn or deserve the gift; we just accept it and it is life changing. Like the prisoner set free, we are called to live a grateful and love-filled life honoring the gift we were given. This is the basis of Christians' actions. What people believe in their hearts defines who they are. Action is a result of what is in the heart. However, as we all know, every one of us has a heart. Those of us with a faith in God above also exhibit similar actions. We believe. What we believe in manifests differently for different people. I see many people who claim to believe, and then they are scrutinized for what they say and what they do.

Only two people have any idea about the faith you have in your heart; that's you and God. You know what you feel. You can sense what is right and wrong. When you do or say something wrong, you feel it in your heart. That's God speaking to you. He is not giving up on you; he is simply reminding you that maybe this isn't a good idea or that is the wrong thing to say.

So let's look at my faith. From the time I was small, I believed in God and knew I was being led by him. Rarely did I express my faith publicly. I was not raised in an evangelistic church, so I am not comfortable raising my hands or praising God with audible amens or hallelujahs. There is nothing wrong with those displays of praise and faith; I just learned a more private and conservative approach. Over time I've learned to have an appreciation for various forms of praise and worship. I believe that everyone has their own distinct way(s) to praise God. Somewhere along the way, I learned about having a personal relationship with my creator. I can't remember specifically how I learned to pray, but I remember praying from a young age. My first memory of prayer was before bedtime as a young child. I learned about God in church and that he was the Creator and that his Son died for us. I remember praying every night before going to bed and before every big event in my life. I remember praying for people to be safe. I learned Bible lessons in Sunday school and youth group. I always prayed. I can't recall spiritual specifics or aha moments, but I remember feeling God's presence in every aspect of my life.

Over the years, my parents have been there for me. However, your parents cannot be with you all the time. They do not make all your decisions for you as you grow up and start to live your own life. I have always felt my Father in heaven's presence in a very real way. There were times when I would find myself in challenging situations, but I was always quick to ask God what I was supposed to learn from the experience. And I *always* got some kind of response. This response was not usually an actual audible reply but more of a feeling in my heart. As I moved through high school and headed off to college, my faith again reminded me that God was with me. I believed in God, and he believed in me. Through all the tough times, I knew God was always watching out for me. I didn't live recklessly, but I knew he had my back.

My mom remembers once when I was seven and I went missing on an outing to the local mall. She became frantic for a time, until she finally located me. I was in the middle of a group of kids. I was playing pinball and winning. Several of the kids were much older and my mom was amazed I was so at ease among them. She tells me I was bigger than most children my age and that might have contributed to my confidence. But she noticed something else. She tells me she has always seen leadership and charisma developing. Forty years later she says my story has lightened her spirit and calmed her own fears about death. What an amazing opportunity; to encourage the person who guided me so carefully in my faith as a child.

As a kid my mom made sure Kim and I were very active in the church. In the summer, we were always enrolled in Vacation Bible School (VBS). We both loved it. In addition to VBS, I also attended the church youth group every week. Kids my age met weekly, and we talked about God and faith. During one of our youth group meetings, our group was approached by another Bible study group. In this group were several of our parents. The "parental" group was led by our pastor. We were led by our youth group leader. I sensed something was brewing when our pastor asked us if we understood evolution versus creation. I remember immediately stepping forward, saying, "Yes, I get it." Our pastor smiled as he explained that he wanted to have a debate between our group (the kids) and his group (the parents). The debate would be moderated and judged by the elders of the church. The topic? Evolution versus creation. I stepped forward another step and on behalf of the kids, I simply said, "We're in." The pastor then stepped forward with two pieces of folded paper in his hands. He told me that one piece of paper had the letter *E* on it, while the other paper had the letter *C* on it. "If you pick *E*, your position is in support of evolution," he stated. "If your paper has a *C* on it, you support creation."

So there I was, heavily involved in a Christian church; I had no doubts at all about faith. At twelve years old, I reached out and grabbed a piece of paper. I immediately retreated to the safety of my group of kids and unfolded the paper. It took me a moment to realize I was looking at the letter *E*. We were tasked with supporting evolution. I looked at the kids in the group and said, "I got this."

Sometimes faith can get clouded by the power of wanting to win—wanting to achieve the top spot. I was twelve, even though I didn't really believe in evolution I knew the arguments well and I wanted to win. Above all else, I felt that burning desire for victory. We prepared and we presented. My case was solid. I was scientific. On completion of the debate, the pastor spoke with the elders. He then stepped forward and said, "The kids won; they had a better argument." Celebration ensued. All the kids went crazy. All except me. I said I had to go to the bathroom, and away I went. In the bathroom, I bowed my head and asked for God to forgive me. I put winning the debate in front of what my true feelings were. I felt terrible. At twelve years old, I realized that as important as winning was to me, winning would never pass the importance of my faith. God forgave me immediately. It is critical to understand that when someone asks for forgiveness of God *and* means it, he will forgive. Lesson learned.

We all make mistakes. Only one person ever existed that was mistake free. His name was Jesus Christ. I am no exception when discussing sin. I have sinned numerous times in numerous situations. I can tell you that sin will cause that funny feeling in your insides. Sin takes on so many different forms. Ironically, people are quick to judge. What one person might view as sin, another might see as behavior that is acceptable to God. We know what God will accept. People of faith know what will disappoint God. People of faith know right from wrong. When one accepts Christ as our Savior, I believe there is a level of understanding that is instantly planted in our souls. Even as children, we feel differently when we do or say something that turns on that feeling inside. The beauty is that God forgives. God hears every one of our prayers and he forgives. It's really up to us to live a life that demonstrates understanding that sin is everywhere and we must do the best we can to resist. When we find ourselves in a bad spot, we can ask for guidance and forgiveness and move on. God knows we are not perfect. This is by design. If we were perfect, we would never have to ask for forgiveness. If we were perfect, we would need God less. Sin is put on this earth for believers and non-believers to experience and then see the glory of God's grace and forgiveness. When used in the right way, this paves the way for us to take in the Holy Spirit and have it guide us. It's worked for me. I hope it works for you.

CHAPTER 3

Books and Baseball

Mom worked with my sister, Kim, and me all of the time. My mother is one of the smartest people I know, and she shared her knowledge with us. Both my sister and I learned the value of education early and excelled in school. That was a result of our mother teaching us the necessary things to succeed.

Each one of us feels and understands success in his or her own way. Many people define success by obtaining material things; I don't. I define success by what has been accomplished. Have I completed what I set out to do? If not, can I still get there? Mom taught us about the importance of setting goals and achieving them. She also taught us the value of learning from our failures. Regardless, my sister and I learned these lessons growing up: how to stay humble in defeat and how to be gracious in victory. These would be key learning concepts for me as I grew up.

My father was instrumental in teaching me how to be an athlete. He had been a football player in college. He taught me that the opportunity to simply play is special. I recall being in the backyard with him when he first put a baseball bat in my hands. I was probably four years old. He intentionally handed me a full-sized wood bat. My fingers barely wrapped around the handle near the knob at the end of the bat. I tried to raise it to swing. I had no chance. The bat was so big, and I was so small. I turned in my frustration and asked what I could do to swing the bat. He told me to "choke up," meaning that I needed to move my hands up the handle toward the barrel. Once I got my hands high enough, the bat was counterbalanced, and I was able to swing. I was so excited! That was the beginning of my approach to all things in life that seemed to have insurmountable odds. There is always a way to overcome the difficulties in life. At that moment, I just wanted to play baseball, and my dad was there to teach me.

My dad taught me about being the best. He said that if you decide to be the best at something, you have to do the things that will get you there. He told me that I had natural gifts and that the only way to become the best was to set goals, work hard, and keep getting better. Dad taught me through his actions, but there was only so much time he could give me. He told me at a very young age, "If you want to be the best, it starts with being better than everyone else on your particular team. Then you have to find out who is the best in the league, and you have to work harder to be better than that person." He said, "It doesn't stop there. You also have to be the best in the area. Find out who that is and watch that person. Practice harder." I didn't understand what he was saying at the time. But I certainly do now.

Never—and I mean never—did my father ever make

me play or practice. I wanted to be the best. I wanted to do whatever I needed to do to make that happen. My father was teaching me a life lesson. To be the best, I understood I would have to work for it myself. How many people challenge themselves long before someone else does? I always look for the best person to measure myself against. I try to figure out a way to outwork the person, be better, and then stay there as long as I possibly can. These life skills that both Mom and Dad taught me were instrumental in how I went on to live my life.

As I entered my school-age years, I realized something very quickly. God had given me special gifts. As a child, we are not able to see those gifts. But now I look back and recognize that my parents—both of my parents—empowered me to be self-motivated and determined. My parents were the gifts. I recognized early on that my academic ability (thanks to Mom) and my athletic desire (thanks to Dad) were special. People always politely say that children are gifted. I had the gift of loving parents who understood the value of work ethics in the academic and athletic arenas. I wanted to be the best. They wanted me to be the best; it was a good combination. Parents have many roles in raising a child. I know that sounds like an overused phrase, but do parents really understand this? Today's parents are developing the next generation.

I went to school in a town of about five thousand people. Gas City Indiana was a farming town right in the middle of the state. The primary employers in our town were glass factories. Generation after generation of people worked in those places. By the end of the 1980s, glass bottles began to fade away. The factories closed. My city reduced in size. As

13

families moved on, some of my friends went away as well. However, some things never went away. Sports were still there, and I played them—all of them.

Starting at about six years old, I decided that I wanted to be with my dad when he coached baseball. I became the bat boy for the Marion Federal Phillies in the little league of Gas City. I was thrilled about my role and more excited to be around some awesome baseball players. Those guys on that little league team were heroes to me. Tracy, Donnie, Eddie— all much older and all very influential. I was still young, but I wanted to be there. Every chance I got, I played with those guys. I watched them. I listened to my dad coach them. When my turn to play came, I was ready.

In my town, little league consisted of nine-to-twelve-year-olds. Understand that when a nine-year-old stands next to a twelve-year-old or when a twelve-year-old is pitching and a nine-year-old is hitting, things get a tad scary. I was terrified, but I realized that the only way to conquer the fear was to face it and let it play out. That lesson was to surface many years later in my life. I made it through the years of little league as well as youth basketball (huge in Indiana), youth football, golf, bowling, and more. I just loved to play and loved to win. As I was growing up in sports, I found myself surrounded by kids who were as passionate as I was about the game—any game. My friends, like me, just wanted to win. Something special was developing.

CHAPTER 4

Team Sports

It was at this point that I made an interesting discovery about myself. I realized that teams win, and teams lose. I didn't really spend much time in individual sports. I played on teams—good teams. When we won, I was elated. I didn't care if I played well or not. I celebrated the joy of victory. Now we didn't win all the games, but I realized that when we lost, I was miserable. At the young age of thirteen, I realized that life is not about the individual. It was not about me. It was about *us*. How did *we* do? Did *we* win? To this day, I structure my life around the success of my team. I don't ever take the credit when we win. I take all the responsibility when we lose. I am the leader. Success is defined by the actions of my team. Failure is determined by my ability to lead my team. I hated when my team lost; it was my fault. I loved when my team won; it was their glory. Leadership was beginning to evolve.

My freshman year at Mississinewa High School was interesting, to say the least. Grades came easy. Thanks, Mom! Our class got to high school, and we were exposed to a losing varsity football team and a losing varsity basketball team; the baseball team was just okay. I didn't know many of the upper classmen, but I knew the kids in my class. I knew that we'd *never* had a losing season in anything, and we sure weren't going to start losing now. During freshman year, we had winning seasons in all sports. People began to see a class of young men who celebrated wins together and lamented over losses together. We were close on and off the field. I never had the privilege of growing up alongside a brother. These wonderful young men became my brothers; they were then and most certainly are now. There were kids on our teams who had no fathers around, and their moms worked double shifts. Those kids were warriors. They were pure athletes.

I didn't see it at the time, but I learned a lesson that would help me shape the lives of my children. Dads, good men to the core, stepped in and became surrogates to those without active fathers. I witnessed it then, but it didn't register. The value of parents who are there for their kids is immeasurable. We were winners. As our tight knit group of athletes moved through high school, we won at all levels. *We* won. And yes, *we* lost. These lessons became fundamental principles in my life. People looked to me for leadership, and I gave it. Integrity was fundamental to my life. What you do when no one is looking speaks volumes about a person's integrity. I was surrounded by people who felt the exact same way.

It was on my high school basketball team that I picked up a nickname that has stayed with me over the years. Our team was young but very aggressive. We were far from winning every game, but we were tough and our opponents felt it. We were determined to improve however, as Indiana has always been known for basketball excellence. Despite my 6'3" frame, I was still considered a small person to be playing "inside" positions. This was one of my advantages however as I was usually underestimated by the opponent. On the court, I played aggressively and in keeping with my passion to win, I was relentless protecting the inside. If you were brave enough to try to score on the inside, you were going to have to face me. One particular game I was fiercely protecting the "paint" (this is the area referred to as the inside of the box closest to the basket). My opponent was visibly frustrated at multiple failed attempts to score when he blurted out *"Man Mike! You hammered me"*. That's all it took. From then on, I was known as Mike, *the hammer*, Mitchener. This nickname followed me to baseball as well as I threw hard pitches and hammered the ball out of the park whenever I could.

When we graduated high school in 1985, my class was recognized as one of the most successful athletic classes ever and the most successful academic class. We had four students who had a 4.0 GPA. All four were active in sports and other extracurricular activities. They gave back to the school and our community; Paul, Shellie, Kris, and Rod were extraordinary people in high school, and they continue to exemplify what it means to be good students and, more importantly, good citizens. I was inspired by the students at Mississinewa High School. To this day, I still see them as some of the most influential people in my life. One hundred and fifty people were in my graduating class. I knew them all, and all of them were special.

CHAPTER 5

What's Next?

After high school graduation came one of the toughest decisions of my eighteen years on the planet. It was time to decide what I wanted to do next. I had options. I was born and raised in Gas City, as was my dad, his dad, and his dad's dad. See where I am going with this? I didn't want to leave. It was all I knew and all I cared to know. Dad pushed me. He wanted something different for me. Constantly he told me to "see the world." Now understand that people don't leave the safe lives they have lived in Gas City. There is comfort there. Dad wanted me to see more, and so did I.

I received a letter in the mail the summer after my senior year. The United States Air Force Academy had offered me a spot in the class of 1989. I didn't even know there was an Air Force Academy. I didn't know that Dan Quayle (vice president for the first President Bush) had selected me to receive a nomination until the letter arrived. On learning about the Academy, taking my first plane ride ever to Colorado Springs, and hanging out with college baseball players, I made my decision; I didn't go. After tossing and turning all night, at the ripe old age of eighteen, I passed on that opportunity. Mom and Dad were not really happy, and I understood why. I was passing on the chance of a lifetime. I have so much respect for the military. Because of the military, I have the freedom to basically live as I see fit. However, I had never once considered selecting the military as a potential career. Having lived in one small town my whole life, I just couldn't see myself in that nomadic lifestyle.

It was then that I began to realize it was time to grow up. My parents told me that they had enough money to pay for one year of college at Indiana University. The rest would have to be covered by student loans and financial aid. I remember sitting at my kitchen table with my parents. They showed me a passbook savings account. "This is all we have for your college; are you sure you don't want to rethink the Academy?" they said. I took the passbook savings account, closed it, and softly passed it back to my parents. I told them that I loved them and that I wanted to do this myself. I explained I would work my way through school by using loans, financial aid, or whatever it took. I said, "Use this for my sister's college." I wasn't sure exactly how I would pay for college. I didn't have a solid plan. But even in my uncertainty, I had faith. The very next day, I received a recruiting letter from a small school in Savannah, Georgia. They wanted me to play basketball and baseball. What kind of offer was it? It was a full scholarship. God's involvement? No doubt. So I signed to play for Armstrong State College.

The summer of 1985 was a tough time for me. As mentioned,

I had a big decision to make regarding where I was going to attend college. Tougher though was the fact that my dad's brother, Frank, was very sick with Hodgkin's disease. I vividly recall going to the hospital to see my uncle. He was dying. My uncle was like a second father to me, and at age forty-three he was rapidly dying, before our very eyes.

He died three days before I was to load up and go to college. Again, I was faced with a difficult decision. My dad and his brother were very close. I realized at the time that if my father was going to take me to college, he would have to miss his brother's funeral. What do you do? I was eighteen years old, and quite honestly, I had never really been away from the comforts of Gas City. After much consideration and some lengthy conversations with my mom, I made the decision to get myself to Georgia from Indiana. I knew that I was going to miss my Uncle Frank's funeral, but I wasn't going to create a situation where my dad would miss his brother's funeral. I was to leave early the next day. Because of that, I went to bed early the night before. Shortly after I drifted off to sleep, my father, who rarely ever woke me up, came into my room. A man of few words, my dad simply said that I was his son, his eldest. He stated that he had waited his whole life to see his kids go off to college. He also told me that he was holding his brother in his arms and felt him take his very last breath. He told his brother that they would be together again one day. He told me that as much as it hurt, he said good-bye to his brother at that moment. I was moved to tears. I was so sad to lose my uncle, but watching my father describe his last moments with his brother and his complete faith in the future for both of them was overwhelming. His faith was demonstrated to me that night. His confidence about reuniting with his brother in heaven was so obvious. But another thing was obvious—his commitment to his family and his clear priorities. What my father was showing me was to *always* commit to your family. They are your legacy. What a valuable lesson my dad taught me that night. Who could possible know that nearly thirty years later, my own faith and family would be so important. So we loaded up and headed off to a new adventure. Georgia, here we come.

The memory of my uncle stays with me even today. In college I played baseball. To my coaches' credit and to the credit of older players who played at Armstrong, we were always allowed to have a team meeting "down the line" prior to the start of the game. Captains would talk about the importance of playing as a team and winning. Then we would say the Lord's Prayer together. It was a tradition to place each hand on the shoulder of the other teammate, and the captains would start the prayer, and then other players would join in. It was a sign of a team. It was a sign of faith. I'll never forget those times. After completing the Lord's Prayer, each player was given the opportunity to "do their own thing." Some would immediately run back to the dugout. Others would begin running sprints in the outfield. Some would start playing catch. My routine *never* wavered. From day one it did not change. I didn't move from where I was at the end of the prayer. I didn't even open my eyes. I kept praying. I prayed the same message each time: "Uncle Frank, I know you're watching me play this game. Watching like you always did when I was in Indiana. I'm playing for you. Stay with me; I know you're there." I said this prayer before every game I played from the time Frank died until I retired from baseball in 1991. He saw every game. He saw every inning. I am certain of that.

CHAPTER 6

College Life

College started for me in the fall of 1985. I had never been to Savannah prior to Mom and Dad loading me up for the trip. I was going far away from the comforts and lifelong familiarity of Gas City. As a freshman I learned about balancing school, athletics, and missing home. Needless to say, like many others I struggled with that balance. Nonetheless I managed to get through my first year of college. Returning to Gas City over a break, I recognized that life was happening. I realized that I belonged in Savannah. There wasn't going to be a "home for the summer" time for me. I stayed a few days and headed back to Savannah. No job. No place to stay. Here I go. Arriving back in Savannah for the summer, I found an apartment to rent from some soccer players who were home for the summer. I also got a job at the local Coke plant in Savannah.

Fall rolled around, and I found myself back in school, back on the baseball team, and back in the grind. This time I had some experience under my belt. The fall season came, and our baseball team rocked. In school I figured out college with a 4.0

the first quarter, a 4.0 the second quarter, and a 3.5 the third quarter. Coupled with a great year in baseball, I began to settle in. I led the nation in RBIs (runs batted in). Competing at the highest level (NCAA I) and achieving that type of recognition might cause someone to be overly confident and maybe even cocky. Not me. All I cared about was one thing: winning. And we won. The team I played on at Armstrong State in 1987 was one of the best teams ever. Like me, the players on that team just wanted to win. And we did. By the end of that season, our small division I baseball team was one of the best teams in the country. We were in the top ten in many different categories (RBIs, batting average, wins, runs per game). We were fueled by one thing: the desire to win.

I spent the summer after my sophomore year in Atlanta. I played on a very talented summer team. We were good. Very good. I had a coach who was a former major league pitcher. He saw that I could throw pretty hard but didn't really know how to "pitch." He taught me. He taught me well. I was in a league that had many former pros and several college stars from all levels. As always, my goal was winning, and we did win. On returning to college for my junior season, I had picked up about five miles per hour on my fastball. I still could hit well, but the arm was in very good condition. I became a candidate for the major league baseball draft. My junior season defined me. I was solid in school, solid on the field, and solid on the mound. By 1988 I was captain of the team. The leader I always practiced being. I worked hard to inspire my teammates in the same manner that my father and those mentors in Gas City had inspired me. I was at the top of my game. I was solid.

I was strong. Bob Seger's "Like a Rock" was on the radio and it became my theme song. That year, I was awarded first team All American status for the position designated hitter. I later learned that I was the first baseball player in Armstrong's history to be awarded this honor. I was ready.

CHAPTER 7

Professional Baseball

I was drafted in the third round of the 1988 professional baseball draft. When drafted as a junior, you have a choice to make; sign a contract and forgo the senior season to play ball or go back to college for one more year. No one from my college had ever been drafted that high before. I never had the desire to play baseball as a professional. I played ball for the love of the game. That's it. I wanted to use baseball as a way to pay for my college. I had promised my parents that, and I delivered. Now I was in unchartered waters.

I negotiated the deal with the team that drafted me. I had one priority, that my education would be funded. Immediately, I was offered a deal where the major league scholarship fund would pick up my college tuition. In essence, major league baseball would now be paying for the completion of my college education. I would play pro baseball in the spring and summer, and I would go to school in the fall and winter. It helped me fulfill the promise I gave my parents. We hammered out a deal, and I signed my contract. Away I went.

Major League Baseball is the governing body for all professional baseball. However, the majority of all baseball players start their professional careers in the minor leagues with aspirations to make it to a major league team. Minor league baseball is an interesting concept. It was in 1988, and it is today. There are players with varying degrees of desperation. Some guys are in it because they have nothing else but baseball. If they don't make it to the majors, life will be hard for them. Other guys play because the timing is right. They might already have their college degrees, or they might be close. Nonetheless, every player wants a taste of the show. The show is the majors. I was the guy who played because I got a chance. Baseball for me was only used as a way to pay for my college. I used baseball at a professional level as a means to do something cool and, most importantly, to finish college. I played three years, and during that time won a Midwest League championship with the South Bend White Sox. I made a ton of friends I still talk with today. Baseball was a beautiful game then, and it is today. It will always stand the test of time as a symbol of the fabric of America. Throw the ball, catch the ball, and hit the ball. It's a simple game that I will always love. We all have to stop playing for one reason or another, but we never have to stop loving the game. Seeing the talented players play the game now reminds me of the talented players I saw then. I loved the game of baseball when I was a six-year-old kid, loved it in high school and college, loved it when I played as a professional, and I will love baseball for the rest of my days. Baseball is the perfect blend of individual and team talent.

CHAPTER 8

Sam's Club

I left the game in 1991. I had graduated from college (mission accomplished) and had gotten married. It was now time to put my college degree to work. I had graduated in 1990 and had given serious consideration to continuing my education. I wanted to be an attorney. I wanted to represent the same guys I had met playing the game I loved. But just about then, an interesting thing happened. Life didn't quite happen the way I had planned. Someone told me a company called Sam's Club was hiring. I was told that it would be a good way to help pay for my law school education. I interviewed and got hired as a manager. They asked me if I wanted to live in the Carolinas or Atlanta. Atlanta used to be my home, and it was about to be my home again. So in October of 1991, I began my career at Sam's Club. That was one of the best decisions I ever made. Sam's Club has been very good to me. It is a remarkable company.

I started my management career in Duluth, Georgia, having no retail management experience. I was just ready to learn. I was blessed with some of the very best people in the world to work for and learn from. My first manager was a guy named Ed Lockhart. Ed and I are still friends to this day. Ed taught me the technical side of the business. He taught me how to read financial reports, how to make decisions that will drive results, and how the retail world ticks. Our Sam's Club in Duluth was run like a well-oiled machine. We made mistakes, but we always learned from them and became better. I did a short stint with Ed (about a year and a half), and then I was asked to go to Austell, Georgia, which is a suburb of Atlanta.

Austell was run by a guy named Arch Watson. Arch was a great manager. Like me, he was an athlete. He was sharp. He always dressed to the nines. Little did I know that Arch would become instrumental in my ability to handle people. Arch was brilliant at making people feel good about the job and, more importantly, about themselves. Arch was notorious for making "the call." He would call employees at home in the early morning and wake them up. He would direct them to kiss their spouses, who were asleep, whisper in their ears that they loved them, and then insist that they take the day off only if they were able to spend it with their families. Those calls didn't come often, but somehow Arch knew the right time for each person. Every time those calls were made to us, Arch knew we needed family time. Arch helped to shape my management style and is still a very close friend to this day.

CHAPTER 9

Becoming a Father

I was put on this earth to be a father. I know that. It is by far my most important responsibility. It was then. It is now. My first child was born while I was an assistant manager in Atlanta. Instantly I knew that my job was not that of a manager but that of someone in charge of leaving the world a little better place than I found it. I was inspired to do that by being a good father. The ways in which you inspire children define you. Being a parent is hard work. It requires discipline, structure, and mental toughness. But when done right, it truly defines you. I believe that some people remember you based on your parenting. If you aren't blessed with children of your own, you can be a surrogate parent to others.

My daughter, Victoria, was born in July 1993. My world was absolutely turned upside down. This wasn't a bad thing. As a matter of fact, it was the best thing that had ever happened to me. She was a tough baby. Parents and surrogate parents know what I'm talking about. Babies take on a personality right away, and first-time parents sometimes struggle from a lack of experience. Your first child takes you to places you've never imagined going. I was blessed with individual time with Victoria that I didn't get with my other children. My bond with Victoria would be tested over twenty years later in a hospital room in Daytona Beach, Florida.

CHAPTER 10

Career Growth

Shortly after Victoria's birth, I was promoted to the position of general manager of Sam's Club. This position was a totally different animal. I was in charge of an entire store. The man who promoted me in 1994 was Dave Davidson. To this day, Dave and I are very close friends. He is a mentor to me in more ways than just professionally. Dave is the kind of person who defines loyalty. In one of his first visits to my store when I became a club manager, Dave showed up on a Saturday morning.

Now, as a club manager, that building is yours. Everything in it is your responsibility. We walked the store, and it wasn't good. Floors were not good. Merchandise presentation wasn't good. I was crushed. I wanted it to be good for him, for my associates, and for my members. It wasn't. After Dave toured my building, he asked me if I could meet him in the parking lot. I was worried that he was going to take my keys and wish me well. What Dave did will forever be etched in my mind. He asked me if there was another manager in the building who could watch over things. There was, and then he asked me to drive to a local convenience store. When we pulled in to the store, he said to go inside and buy him two Gatorades. Perplexed by his request, I complied. On coming back to the car, he asked me to drive him to a certain place in Atlanta that was close to the interstate. It was just an empty lot. We parked, opened the Gatorades, and just sat there. It seemed like an eternity. Finally Dave said, "You know, I believe in you; you are the right person to run that store." We didn't talk about all the things that needed to be fixed. We didn't talk about what was wrong. He just knew what I needed to hear. I'll never forget those thirty minutes. They changed me. When things are rough, the leader is supposed to step up and lead. He can't lead with fear and intimidation. He leads with what it takes to motivate. Dave knew what I needed. After we finished talking, Dave asked me to drive him back to the store. He then instructed me to head to my house, change clothes, relax, and "bring it" on Monday. I did just that. Little did I know but nearly twenty years later—when I was in trouble again in a hospital room in Daytona Beach—Dave would be there, believing in me again.

After a year as a club manager in Atlanta, I was asked to relocate my family to sunny Sarasota, Florida, where a club needed a manager. It was a great opportunity, a great club, and a great place to live. Don Nickens would be my new boss. I relocated my family to Bradenton, Florida, in the fall of 1995. I was now a resident of the sunny state of Florida. Our family added two boys while we were there. Life was moving fast. Don Nickens was a very experienced manager. He had many years of service with the company; I didn't. He had culture; I didn't. Don would go on to become the most important person in my Sam's Club career. He was tough on me. I happened to be "blessed" to be the manager of his home club. Every Friday Don would come in to work, nod his head, and get prepared to tour my building with me. Don's skill set is complex to many but simple to few. I was one of the lucky people who understood the simplicity of this business. He believed in building a team, a team that you could rely on. He also believed that not understanding this team concept meant struggling in his market. Being a former athlete, this belief rang true to my core. Don built a tremendous team. He was always there to lift us up when we were down and push us when we needed to be pushed. He believed in celebrating together. He believed in helping each other in rough times. To this day, I still call Don Nickens when I need some encouragement. He was my friend then, and he is my friend now.

In 2001 I was promoted to district manager and relocated to the Denver area. I was excited to make the move and further my career. We packed up and headed west. We were blessed with our fourth child, Sarahbeth, and life appeared to be wonderful. It wasn't. Soon we realized that Denver was not the home we needed. I worked around the clock, and I lost sight of what I was cut out to do. I remember one particular Sunday morning when I woke up early to get some Sam's Club work done. I fired up my laptop at about five in the morning while all the family was still sleeping. I told myself that I could get my work done long before the kids woke up. At noon my son walked up to me and asked if I was still going to play ball with him in the yard. At that moment I knew I needed to make a change. We headed back to Florida after a year and a half in Denver. Denver is a wonderful town. I never got to see it. I was committed to being good at what I did. Again, I looked for the best and tried to emulate what they did. It finally dawned on me that I needed the structure of a store manager's position. My family needed me to be at home, and that was my priority.

Back to Florida. This time we landed in Daytona Beach. It was 2003, and I had something to prove. Although I failed as a district manager, I wanted to show anyone who was looking that I was a talented manager. I had been trained well. My family and I decided that this was to be the place to raise all the kids. We were going to lock in to this area and raise a family. Making a decision like that was big. It required a team approach. We did just that, and so by 2004 our house was built and we moved into our quiet neighborhood. Around that time I was informed that my Armstrong jersey, number 25 was to be retired. Mine was the second jersey retired in the last 75 years. What an honor. Looking back on my past was fun, but I was looking forward now. I had big plans for myself and my family. God had other plans.

CHAPTER 11

The Curve Ball

Things happen. They do. I wanted to stay married forever, raise my kids, watch my grandchildren come, and grow as a person and as a family. Sometimes things just don't work out as planned. In October 2011 my wife and I divorced. I was shattered beyond words. It was around that time when I realized that God had a plan for me. After numerous attempts to get the marriage back on track, my wife told me she wanted to end it. Karen is a great mother, and she comes from a great family. We put in twenty years of life together and had four beautiful kids. We still work together very well in supporting each other and raising our children.

Shortly after learning my marriage was to end, I decided to fly to Indiana to visit with my parents. They had been married for almost forty-five years, and I needed help understanding what was happening. They tried—they really did—but I was inconsolable. I wanted what they had. Through thick and thin, they stayed together. Side by side, they handled all things that came their way. Even though I knew my marriage was ending, I needed them to lift me up. But nothing seemed to work. I was broken.

I drove myself to Louisville around five in the evening. I had a flight early the next morning back to Florida. I checked into a motel and settled down for the evening. *I got this,* I kept telling myself. After dinner, I walked back to the hotel, changed into some bed clothes, and watched a little basketball on TV. *I got this.* I tried to just unwind, but I felt my mind getting away from me. How am I going to do this? What about my children? How am I going to balance work and family alone? I was feeling shaky. I shut the TV off around eleven thirty that night to try to get some sleep. I couldn't sleep. My mind was racing, and I was slowly losing control. I turned the TV back on to watch a few old reruns. *I got this,* I kept telling myself. I was beginning to get warm, so off came the bed clothes, on came the air conditioning down as far as it would go, and back to bed I went. I had to get some sleep. About two in the morning I finally got out of bed. I was drenched in sweat, and I was in trouble. My mind wouldn't let go. I was completely out of control, and I was feeling desperate. Gone was the confident, cocky All American, baseball captain, *hammer,* who easily sailed through life. Gone was the assurance that my faith was all I needed. I stood up from the bed and resigned myself to the fact that I could no longer live like this anymore. I had never felt this way before, and I sure didn't want to feel this way again. There are two ways out from such an experience. I wanted the easy way. So for about two minutes, in a motel in Louisville, Kentucky, I wanted to end my life. This is a classic example of Satan having his arms wrapped around me. He had convinced me that the pain I was feeling was not worth living. As I tried to figure out how to end it, I felt hands on my shoulders—strong hands, big hands. These hands pushed me down to my knees. At that moment I felt the need to pray. I don't know why, but I did. After I was done, I realized what was happening. There was a battle for my soul between God and Satan. God won. I ended my prayer, smiled, lay down, and slept. When I awoke a few hours later, I was refreshed. God stepped in. God saved me. He works in wonderful ways. He does. Some people may consider his work coincidental. Others may say it's just "luck." I call it faith. The power of faith is immeasurable.

My cousin, Chris, is my age. He and I grew up together in Gas City. We played all types of sports together. We were like brothers. Chris is a very good Christian man, and he exemplifies his faith daily. For some reason, we had lost touch. He was still in Indiana, raising his four kids, and I was in Florida, raising mine. On the way to the airport the next day, I received a call from an Indiana number. I thought it was a bit strange because it was early in the morning, so I answered the call. Chris was on the phone, and he was surprised that I was up that early to answer. He told me that he and his family were on the way to Florida, and he was hoping that we could see each other. Just a few hours earlier, I was on the verge of ending my life. Now one of the most influential Christian men I had ever known was on the phone with me, wanting to see me. I hadn't seen Chris in years and now this? We made plans to meet. I hung up the phone. I looked up and said, "Thank you."

God was there; he was in my heart. As broken as I still was, Chris—through the power of the Word—helped me. He got me refocused on what was important. Chris stayed with me for a few days and got me moving in the right direction. He is a man of God. He was speaking God's Word. After our time together ended, I said, "I got this." But this time, I meant "God's got this."

CHAPTER 12

Faithfulness

Life was happening to me. Life is a chaotic blend of wonderful things that happen, with the occasional bad event as well. Faith or beliefs, whatever they may be, and God's faithfulness provide guidance through both good and bad times. God knows what is going to happen. He does. It has already been determined. I speak about destiny from pure opinion. I never try to push my thoughts on others. I was gifted by God with the ability to talk to people. Regardless of who the person is, I can connect with him or her. It is a gift.

Raised in a Christian church, I learned about faith at a very young age. Sometimes kids go through the motions of church just to please their parents. They don't really understand the traditions and meaning of faith until something happens in their lives that can only really be explained by or endured through faith. I was no exception. I didn't mind going to church and was involved in Sunday school and youth group. At twelve years of age, I was baptized into the Christian faith, having made my own decision to follow Christ. I had a habit of praying at night and kept this habit into adulthood. As captain of the baseball team in college, I led the players in prayer. My faith remained, and I continued to grow and learn and always felt God was close to me. I'm sure many people have felt God in their lives and have seen his works so often. I recall his direct protection of me once when I was about to pull out on a busy highway. I was in college at the time, driving with a friend in a hurry, when something told me to press the brakes. As I did, a car I had not noticed barreled passed us at seventy miles per hour. I never saw the car, and neither had my passenger. We had escaped a direct hit and certain death. I am sure I have benefited from God's protection surrounding me even when I was not aware of it. God was with me then and remained with me even in my darkest times.

As the trauma of divorce began to consume me, another incredible event took place. Mr. Truett Cathy was a dear friend of mine. He is the founder of Chick-fil-A. Mr. Cathy lived part time in both Atlanta and New Smryna Beach, which is about fifteen miles from Daytona. He shopped in my Sam's Club frequently, and we became good friends. Mr. Cathy was a man of God. He was a kind man who loved children. I was elated that our friendship was so strong. He would invite my family and me to Atlanta to go to his church with him. He was a spiritual mentor to me. Mr. Cathy was never afraid to speak the truth. When I was privileged to be with him, I said very little and listened a whole lot.

I don't remember what day it was, but I do remember the overwhelming grief that consumed me relative to the divorce. I was sitting at Sam's Club, and I was feeling broken.

Marriage is supposed to last a lifetime, and mine was in trouble. I looked up from my seat, and standing in front of me was Mr. Cathy. Now understand that he never came to my Sam's Club without me knowing. Never. But when I was in a very serious moment of despair, there he stood. He asked me if he could sit down and speak with me. He asked me if she (my wife) had given up. I said I felt that she had, and he just looked at me. I had tears in my eyes because my marriage was ending, and I had this wonderful man taking the time to just talk to me. I needed that moment of friendship and fellowship, and he knew it. Mr. Cathy then asked for my cell phone, stepped away, and made a phone call. He returned to the table where I was sitting, handed me my phone back, and then did something that I will never forget as long as I live. He prayed for me. He asked me to hold his hands and look in his eyes, and he prayed for me. Like me, he had tears in his eyes. He told me to not give up. He prayed for me, holding my hands. After completing the prayer, Mr. Cathy asked me to contact his son, Bubba. I called Bubba, and he said that his dad had explained what I was going through. Then Bubba Cathy asked me if he could pray for me. I was speechless. Bubba prayed for me, and then he made a wonderful offer. Parents have a way of influencing their children. This was proof. After speaking with his father, Bubba told me about a marriage counseling program that Chick-fil-A sends their employees to. He told me that when they send people who are having marriage problems to this retreat, there's an 80 percent chance of saving the marriage. I knew that the retreat would be a last ditch effort to save my marriage. I asked Karen about attending, and she declined. At that moment I knew my life was going to be forever changed. Life goes on. God was working out his plan for me. My commitment and willingness was not a question. Hello, new life.

CHAPTER 13

Single Father

I made a life for myself and my kids. My number-one priority will always be my family. After twenty years of marriage, moving forward into the single world was not an easy task. However, I must say that the love of my kids and the support they showed meant the world to me. Being single was new but being part of a family was not. I stayed in my home, and the joint custody thing began to evolve. Life moved fast for me. My children's events didn't suddenly stop. Working full time and committing myself to their events was challenging but not impossible. All my kids were active, and I wasn't about to miss anything. Faith in God somehow always seems to appear when needed. When times seemed hopeless, I prayed. When times were good, I prayed. Before I went to bed, I prayed. Even though I was alone through a divorce, God remained faithful to me. Time and time again, I felt his presence. We had a special relationship, and I knew it.

The divorce was final in October 2011. I began to live a new life. I say this because life as a single divorced dad was not something I had ever planned. There were times of despair as well as times of loneliness, but I had a tremendous group of friends, coworkers who were always there, and a drive that burned inside me. Coupling those things with the power of the almighty Father, I was prepared to move into the next phase of life.

So life went on. I took care of myself. I took care of my family. Just another example of someone who loved God, loved his family, and loved life. Year after year, I began to settle in. I got comfortable. I never took things for granted, and I always prayed. Praying is not difficult. I believe in God and Jesus Christ. I prayed when I was thankful (many times!), and I prayed when things were difficult. People asked me on many occasions, "Are you religious?" I would pause and say, "Well, I believe in God." You see, I believe your actions define you. Was I religious? Am I religious? It's not about my definition, nor is it about a dictionary definition. It's about what you feel in your heart, but more important than how you feel is how you live regardless of how you feel at any given moment. Being religious is a person's way of describing someone else. It's like saying someone is tall, but he or she may only be six feet. You either believe in heaven or you don't. You either believe in God or you don't. I never forced my beliefs on others. I just lived my life with faith; if I could help someone with faith-based issues, I did. Funny, that simple explanation would later become a major factor in my life.

CHAPTER 14

The Unthinkable

Flash forward to September 2014. I had been divorced for nearly three years. I had dated from time to time, and I had begun to rediscover life. However, something was off. Sleeping was becoming more challenging. I wasn't unhappy, but I just felt things were changing. I had just recently driven my son to college about twelve hours away, and maybe that was part of the issue. Nonetheless, I was off. Fortunately (or unfortunately), I had this "I am Mike Mitchener, and I can figure this out" attitude. Some people might describe me as cocky. Some might say I am confident. Either way, I knew I could figure this out. Little did I know what was about to happen. September 11, 2014 was a normal day. It was a Thursday. My schedule at Sam's Club was 9:00 a.m. to 7:00 p.m. I structured this schedule throughout the school year so I could spend the night before with my youngest daughter and then have the privilege of taking her to school the next morning. On this ordinary day I did just that. Dropping her off at school, I kissed her, told her I loved her, and headed off to Sam's Club. It was an uneventful day. Around 5:00 p.m. the closing manager informed me that she would be going out for some dinner. She came back to Sam's Club around 5:30 p.m. and said, "Why don't you head home early?" I declined, but to her credit, she persisted. My managers and I have a special relationship. We tell it like it is. We are honest with each other. We take care of each other. My manager, Ashley, saw something in my eyes, and she knew I needed to get out. After refusing to go home, she suggested I go to the gym. Initially, Ashley asked me if I had trained that morning. Usually—in fact 99 percent of the time—I go to the gym at five in the morning. Also, I train four to five times per week. For some reason, I didn't go to the gym that day. After some consideration, I agreed, and off I went to train at Amped Fitness in Daytona Beach. Training at 5:30 p.m.? His plan was beginning. I finished training about seven in the evening and headed out the door. Something didn't seem right, and the young lady at the front desk noticed. On my way out she asked me if I was okay. I replied to her that I was very dizzy and really didn't know why. I've been going to the weight room for thirty years. I know my body. I know when something is not right. Nonetheless, I headed out the door. My workout was over.

CHAPTER 15

In the Dark

As I left the gym, I crossed in front of a car driven by a young lady name Kayli Cantrell. Kayli saw me, and more importantly, she saw someone who just didn't seem "right." Kayli pulled her car into the parking space right in front of the gym. She got out of her car and looked back to see if I was still "off." I had walked to a relatively remote part of the parking lot. Going to the gym at five thirty in the evening is a lot different than going at five o'clock in the morning. Needless to say, parking is plentiful in the early morning; however, in the evening, close spots are always taken. Upon exiting her car with her bag on her shoulder, Kayli was forced to make a tough decision. She was about fifteen feet from the front door of the gym. Decision time. Go back to the parking lot and check on a strange guy or go work out? She came to check on me. A pretty, young, twenty-three-year-old year old female walked across the parking to check on some guy she didn't know. Was that luck? Fate? God? I'll take the God answer.

On arriving at where she thought I would be, Kayli found

me on all fours. Hidden from anyone else, she asked, "Are you okay?" I replied while holding my chest, "I think I'm having a heart attack."

Guess where Kayli worked? Halifax Hospital in Daytona Beach. Guess what floor? Cardiology. So again, was this luck? Fate? God? Well, again, I'll take the faithful, almighty Father. I have been told by several doctors that if she hadn't come to my aid, I would have died in that parking lot. Kayli saved my life as a result of God's direction. Why would a young lady decide to walk out in a parking lot when she only has ten feet to walk into the gym and start her workout? She walked nearly fifty yards to check on me. Why? Because it was his plan. There's more.

CHAPTER 16

A Series of Miracles

When she found me, Kayli knew there was very little chance of her being able to move me. She might have weighed 110 pounds, and I was tipping the scales at 240. Unsure of what to do because of the circumstances, she raised herself up and looked for help. Enter miracle number two. Kayli saw a guy walking into the gym. He was a big man. Kayli had trained at that time of day at that gym for maybe three years. I had never trained at that gym at that time of day. Kayli later informed me that she had never seen that guy before and has not seen him since the event. Once again, I ask the question. Why did she see him for the first time on that fateful night? Was he an angel put there by God himself? Kayli called out to the man that she needed help, and he came over to assist. According to her, he was well over six feet five inches and appeared to be a bodybuilder. The man picked me up and basically carried me back into the gym.

As my guardian angel was carrying me back into the gym, Kayli sprang into action. Being an employee in cardiology and knowing that I was having cardiac problems, Kayli called in the troops. Call number one went to Dr. Steven Minor. Kayli contacted Dr. Minor at home, as he was on call but not at the hospital. He was having dinner with his wife and children, and Kayli needed him. Actually it was I who needed him, but Kayli was speaking for me. After contacting Dr. Minor, Kayli called other staff who worked in cardiology. All of them answered her call. All of them got ready to go back into the hospital. I needed them, and Kayli knew it. We were battling time.

In the gym I was placed behind the desk, and the ambulance was called. I was still conscious, but I was fading fast. I became sick and vomited, and in the process I aspirated, meaning I inhaled stomach contents into my lungs. Not good. Now my breathing was in trouble, my heart was giving out, and I was fading. Time was ticking away. The ambulance showed up about eight minutes or so after I went down. I was still conscious but in very bad shape. The crew loaded me up on the stretcher and put me in the truck. Time ... Ironically, one of the ambulance crew was a friend of my son, and when he realized who I was, it became very personal to him. He told me later that he was not going to allow his friend's father to die on his watch. About a minute after being loaded up on the ambulance—approximately nine minutes after Kayli found me—life stopped. My heart quit pumping. Life was leaving me. Luckily, I was surrounded by the best medical crew around. They pulled out the paddles and brought me back. Miracle? Yep. God involved? For sure.

Halifax Hospital was one mile from the gym. When I

got there, I was in very bad shape. I was quickly moved to the emergency room, and the staff began to work on me. In the process, my heart stopped again and again and again. Four times in the ER my heart stopped and was restarted. On the last stoppage, after three shocks, things looked very bleak. The ER doctor wanted to hit me a fourth time after that particular stoppage. This procedure is rare, but the staff would not give up. They fired up the paddles and hit me with as much as they could. My heart came back. As close as I came to death, the staff wouldn't allow it to happen. They were absolutely resolved to save me. The young man who knew my son stayed there the whole time. The medical staff wouldn't give up, and neither would I. Finally those dedicated folks in the ER got me stabilized and moved to cardiology. How many people are saved daily in ERs across the world? ER personnel are warriors. Warriors fight. They fight for what they believe in. They are heroes. God still involved? Absolutely.

Up to cardiology I went in extremely critical condition. In the ER they had determined that I had suffered a major heart attack caused by a blood clot that appeared to have landed in the left anterior descending coronary artery (LAD). This is the coronary artery that supplies most of the left ventricle with blood, and the left side of the heart is the one that pumps blood out to the entire body. This artery is so important to delivering life-sustaining blood to the heart muscle itself that a blockage in this area is also known as the "widow maker." But by the time my cardiologist saw me, I was suffering from more than the heart attack. The cardiac arrest meant that I was in cardiogenic shock. Because of multiple pulmonary embolisms (blood clots), I was unable to breathe on my own, and so I had a breathing tube placed in my airway. The cardiologist noted that it was difficult to get an appropriate amount of oxygen into my lungs, and I had a critically low potassium level. For some unknown reason, my potassium level on arrival at the hospital had fallen to 1.6. Normal potassium levels are between 3.5 and 4.5, and as any medical person knows, a potassium level of 1.6 can cause more problems with muscle contraction. I was being given potassium through a tube into my stomach and through my veins while I was being prepped for the cardiologist to try to remove the blood clot in the artery in my heart. The procedure was difficult. After removing the clot, the blood vessel was still not open for blood flow, and so a tiny metal stent was placed to hold the vessel open. Immediately after removing the clot, however, my heart stopped pumping normally again and entered a potentially lethal arrhythmia (called ventricular fibrillation). I had to again have two shocks to get my heart back into a normal rhythm. I have been told there were seven total heart stoppages in about an hour and a half. The normal heart ejects about 65 percent or more of the blood within it with each pump. This is known as the ejection fraction, and it tells the medical staff about the strength of the heart muscle. The cardiologist documented that my ejection fraction was 45 percent at the time of heart attack. The cardiologist decided to insert a catheter into my heart for a hypothermia protocol. This involved lowering my body temperature so that my metabolism would slow and my organs (primarily my brain) would be protected while

I healed—if I healed. My lungs were compromised from the pulmonary embolism (blood clot in my lungs), thus causing less oxygen to get to my brain. This caused a stroke. The cardiologist documented his concerns about the possibility that I would suffer permanent brain damage. All the blood flow and heart rhythm issues created a problem with blood flow to my kidneys, and within hours I was showing signs of acute kidney injury as well. So I suffered a major heart attack, pulmonary embolisms, a stroke, acute kidney injury, and I was having a hard time getting enough oxygen. I was alive, though just barely.

All of this was going on at the hospital as a select group of people were working hard to find my family. This proved to be a difficult task. I was at the gym when my heart attack hit and I never bring my wallet inside. That means my driver's license with my name and address was locked in my truck. All I had with me was my work out clothes and my phone. But I do a lot of work on my phone and so it is locked with a password. Nobody could open it. As a result, for several hours I was a "John Doe" at the hospital. Somehow the last missed call was visible and one of the nurses at the hospital recognized the name. The nurse then was able to get the information to this person who contacted my daughter Victoria. But she was about an hour out of town. In order to remove the "John Doe" status, someone had to assure the hospital staff of my name. That means they had to find someone who would come to the hospital and verify my identity. I was scheduled to play in a golf tournament the next morning and a local friend was to be on my team. He was contacted and was able to positively identify me for the staff. It was not long after that, I am told, that my daughter Victoria arrived and tried for several hours to get in touch with my parents in Indiana. My mom remembers a local police officer coming to my parents' home to notify them that their son was gravely ill. She relays traveling to my sister's home in the middle of the night in order to get a flight out to Florida the next morning. By the time my mom and dad arrived in Florida, many people knew about my hospitalization. My mom remembers the rental car saleswoman at the airport telling her that she knew me and with tears in her eyes hugging my mom in support. Both of my parents were overwhelmed by the number of visitors already at the hospital when they arrived. A friend of mine, Joseph, from Africa, was one of those Christians who shone with God's love. Joseph was visiting me when my parents arrived. My mom describes Joseph bringing them both into my hospital room. While laying hands on me, said the most beautiful prayer my mom had ever heard. She has told me how moved she was by Joseph's beautiful prayer. She recalls his faith shining through in that moment. In that terrible time, Joseph's beautiful faith was enough to sustain my parents during the coming weeks. God was remaining with us all.

As the days went on, I had ongoing problems with breathing. I had the tube and the breathing machine, but each time they tried to wake me up and allow me to breath on my own, I began violently coughing and fighting, and they had to place me back under heavy sedation just to keep the oxygen going into my lungs. At one point, I was placed on a special rotating bed to allow fluid in my lungs to move. Eventually the medical team began to discuss removing the tube from my throat and making an incision in my neck to create a tracheotomy. This was so that I could continue to get breath support from the machine but not suffer damage to my mouth and throat from the tube. In many cases these tracheotomies remain forever in those who cannot breath on their own. They decided to try one more day, but plans were underway for the procedure if I had to remain on the breathing machine. So just imagine the agony my family and friends faced. I was asleep. Alive? Yes. Damaged? More than likely.

I firmly believe that when someone is in a coma, the waiting for others has to be terrible. Questions were asked. How will he be when he wakes up? Will he know us? Many questions. Many possibilities. I just can't imagine my family's angst. Where will we bury him? What about his kids? It must have been terrible. But I know that God was working his plan. His wonderful plan was being executed perfectly.

It's important to understand the numbers here. Most medical professionals know these statistics. I didn't know it then, but I know it now. I will never forget these numbers. Ninety-eight percent of all people who have a widow maker heart attack die. According to my cardiologist, I had ten minutes to get medical attention. Ten minutes. Time passes by quickly. So now if we rewind a little bit and think about Kayli *not* coming back to check on me in that parking lot, I would have died. My first heart stoppage occurred about a minute after I got in the ambulance. One minute! Fate? Nah. God? Yeah. So 98 percent die from the widow maker heart attack. Got that? If you factor in the pulmonary embolism, I lose another 1 percent chance of survival. Then, if you throw in the stroke, I lose about .5 percent chance. The bottom line is I had a .5 percent chance of survival. Of that, .25 percent of the people who survive all these things come back with major physical and or mental disabilities. Some would describe a successful outcome as living out my days in some sort of supervised care facility. So my parents were faced with the fact that my chances of survival were bleak, and if I did make it, I would most likely be forever changed. Those were the numbers given to them. I might never walk or talk or live independently again. I might never even regain consciousness. God had other ideas.

While I was in a coma, my daughter, Victoria, emerged as quite an amazing and capable leader. So many people were worried about me and interested in my recovery that the phone calls must have been overwhelming. Victoria took charge and filed regular updates via a web account. She had no idea at the time, but people all over the country who were worrying and praying for me were hanging on her every update. Later I was told that her poise and ability to convey my critical condition was a welcome lifeline to many of my friends and family. She never lost hope and always presented even unfortunate clinical events in a positive light. With her blessing, her actual entries appear in the following pages. Reviewing these entries and the many comments people added were so special and still inspire and move me today.

Internet Entries by Victoria Mitchener

September 12, 2014, 12:11 p.m.

First off, I would like to say thank you to everyone for the endless phone calls and prayers. As many of you know, my dad suffered a major heart attack last night at his gym but was incredibly fortunate to have a nurse from Halifax Health there to call 911 for him. My mom and I and many other family members and friends are here to support him. We are optimistic that he will have a full recovery. We will know more on Sunday when the doctors awaken him from the medically induced coma. Until then, we would really appreciate prayer. Thank you so much, everyone. I will keep you posted. —Victoria.

September 12, 2014, 3:46 p.m.

We just finished visiting with Dad, and he is still doing okay. We checked in with the nurse taking care of him, and she has let us know that his arrhythmia has gone down pretty significantly since even this morning. She said he is only having irregular heart beats once an hour, and sometimes less. This is great news, since his heart is working completely on its own. They also let us know that once they begin re-warming him to normal body temperature, it will take one hour per one quarter of a degree. So it will be around twenty-four to twenty-eight hours, since he is currently at 91 degrees body temperature. We are thinking around nine in the evening tomorrow he will be awake. Still hoping for the best and we are truly beyond thankful for all of your kind words. —Victoria.

September 12, 2014, 8:17 p.m.

We just left the hospital to head home and collect ourselves. Last update for the night: he is the same as he's been. His color is looking better and better though, and his heart is still working well. There is less arrhythmia, and his heart rate is increasing. God is definitely working for him and keeping him safe. He's also working tirelessly in the hearts and hands of the nurses who have been absolutely wonderful and helpful. I think now the best thing to do is just continue to pray. Things are looking better by the hour, and hopefully by morning we will see more improvements. Everyone, please pray with me to watch over him tonight and to watch over the staff at Halifax Medical. I will post again as soon as I get to the hospital in the morning. —Victoria.

September 13, 2014, 11:14 a.m.

We are here with him in the room now. He is at 97 degrees currently so just one more degree to go! All his signs are looking good. He let out a couple coughs a little while ago. They will begin to wean him off of the paralytic and sedatives soon. Let's pray for a healthy and active brain when he wakes up! —Victoria.

September 13, 2014, 2:33 p.m.

Just another small update for everyone. He is no longer receiving the paralytic, but they still have him heavily sedated. They are moving a few of his lines from his groin to his arm to prepare him for movement. This is a *great* sign. We are so anxious to have our dad back! I also wanted to update everyone on the family. We are hanging in there and staying strong for each other. We are currently on the way to a Pop Warner game to watch Sarahbeth cheer. Would my dad have it any other way? Well, that's it for now. Updates will keep coming as I get them. —Victoria.

September 13, 2014, 5:23 p.m.

Okay, so we are back playing the waiting game. Things were looking better, but he is back to needing the sedatives and has been re-paralyzed. When the doctors took him off the medications, he became agitated and was fighting his tubes. He did open his eyes and move his hands and feet though, and that is a good sign. They are now checking to see if he has any broken ribs or clots in his lungs from the initial CPR. They won't be attempting to wake him up again until tomorrow. We are all emotionally tired from the ups and downs, but we are still praying and hopeful that tomorrow we will see even more improvements. —Victoria.

A message to Mike' Sam's Club family September 13, 2014, 8:24 p.m.

(The below message was posted by Victoria at the request of Matt Hughes after noting the volume of visitors at the hospital)

Sam's Club family, the support each and every one of you is offering is amazing. Please keep Mike in your prayers. As Victoria stated, Mike is still under. I know a number of you are waiting to see him, but I ask each of you to let him rest. As soon as Mike is awake and alert, I will let everyone know." —Matt Hughes.

I would like to add that the support from all of you has been incredible. People from all over the state and the country have been calling and sending prayers. He has been with Sam's for my entire life, and many of you have seen our family grow and have been there for and with us since the beginning. This week has truly shown me what it means to have a "work family." And I know he truly saw and thought of all of you as his family. I can't thank his store in Daytona enough for all that they have done for us—from just being there in general to bringing food and drinks to the hospital and the house, offering rides, saying prayers, and making sure we are taken care of. You all are such amazing people, and I thank God for every single one of you.

As for tonight, they are running some cat scans on him, and he is still in stable condition. We will know the results tomorrow, and hopefully they will try to wake him up again.

We're all ready to have him back! Goodnight, everyone. —Victoria.

September 14, 2014, 8:23 a.m.

Okay, so we have the results from his scans, and they did show a clot in his lungs. This is probably causing him difficulty in breathing, which was a big concern for the doctors when he came off the paralytic and sedative yesterday. He had difficulty breathing on his own, and his oxygen levels went too low for them to feel comfortable. We have some wonderful news though, and that is that he had a flawless brain scan. So no bleeding or major damage there! This was definitely one of my biggest fears, so I was so happy to hear that. The doctors have begun to give him heparin, which is a blood thinner to try to rid him of the lung clot. They will also be checking his legs to make sure there is nothing else causing problems.

We will be heading to the hospital soon for visiting hours around noon. Doctors will not be trying to wake him up until that clot is gone. When I find out when that is, I will definitely let everyone know. Until then, my dad's sister and I will be strictly enforcing the two-at-a-time rule per the request of the nurses who are overwhelmed with questions. These women and men have been very lenient and understanding until now, but I think they need a little time to be able to just focus on my dad. Let's pray for them again today to have clear minds and steady hands as they work on him and get him better. Let's also pray that he has no other clots anywhere in his body and thank the Lord that he protected his brain. —Victoria.

Sep 14, 2014, 5:04 p.m.

Okay! We are making progress. I just spent the last hour with him, and everything is looking positive. He is responding well to the decrease in oxygen on the ventilator, and he is working hard to breathe on his own. They said the blood thinner is working great too. They are seeing a pretty good amount of blood coming from his lungs, so that means the clot is releasing. While I was in there and they were moving him around, he opened his eyes and looked at me. I was talking to him and trying to get him to keep eye contact, and he kept his eyes open for maybe thirty seconds, on and off. It was so relieving to see his eyes again and watch him do something on his own. Things are looking better and better. It's just a matter of finding the happy medium between the sedatives and the oxygen. They are very slowly and very cautiously bringing both down. Keep praying. It's working! —Victoria.

September 15, 2014, 12:49 p.m.

Okay, everyone, I'm sorry that I haven't posted in a while. Everything is still about the same. He had an echocardiogram, and we're waiting on his intensive care doctor to look at it and collaborate with his cardiac doctor on their next step. He does have a pulmonary embolism, and it is apparently pretty big. This could be causing some stress on his heart and vice versa. They may try to remove it. We are avoiding having to use stronger blood thinners because of the risk of hemorrhage in his brain. Other than that, nothing much has changed. He is on 40 percent oxygen on his ventilator, which is an improvement from last night, and his temperature has gone down a little bit. The next step is taking care of this clot in his lung. We are very much anticipating this, and as soon as we know the direction of the doctors' plan, I will let everyone know. —Victoria.

September 15, 2014, 3:20 p.m.

He is off sedatives and responding well. He is hearing our voices and looking at us. He has done a few commands such as "wiggle your toes," "blink if you can hear me," and he has responded to his dad and my brother asking him to squeeze their hands. This is huge! —Victoria.

September 15, 2014, 10:16 p.m.

Sorry, everyone, for the late post again. Today has been a roller coaster of really high highs and pretty low lows. He was responding to our voices earlier, and that was a great sign and very encouraging. It's always a relief to see him try to do things on his own. However, the reason they lowered his sedation was to test how he responded to being taken off the ventilator. The test did not go well, and his doctors had to re-sedate to make him comfortable again. It is frustrating to feel that we take one step forward and two steps back, but I know he is fighting hard, and all our prayers are working. Tomorrow is a new day and another opportunity for improvement. This is how we have to approach this process. All we can do is be there for him and ask God to continue working his miracles on him. Until tomorrow. —Victoria.

September 16, 2014, 11:09 a.m.

Connor and I are on our way to the hospital right now. My Aunt Kim (dad's sister) just got a call from the hospital that they are about to move one of his lines from his groin to a vein in his neck. This is a risky procedure because of the heparin he is on. Pray with us that all goes well. I will update everyone as soon as I know how it went. —Victoria.

September 16, 2014, 4:37 p.m.

Hi, everyone. So we have some great news. The transfer of his lines from his groin to his neck went really well. It was a quick procedure, and we watched the doctor go in and come out. He let us know that everything went very smoothly. No bleeding. That is fantastic! I stopped by around 4:30 p.m., and as soon as I walked up, the nurses were closing his curtain to move a few more of his lines, which they said could take thirty to forty-five minutes, and to come back to visit. I make sure to let him know each time I am there that we are praying for him and are here for him. I think he already knows that though. The doctors also took some ultrasounds on his arms, which showed many clots. This is probably where his pulmonary embolism came from, which is unusual; they normally come from the legs after being sedentary. We all know he was never that! A hematologist is on board now who will be studying him and taking tests of his blood to see if there could possibly be any genetic factors or defects causing this problem. It will probably take a little while to get the results, but when I find anything out I will let you know. All still looks good! I'll be back at the hospital around 8:00 p.m. for the last set of visiting hours, and I will post again when I leave. —Victoria.

September 16, 2014, 10:22 p.m.

Alright, so I talked with the nurse on duty tonight, and she said we are about the same as we've been all day. There is less fluid in his lungs, which is good, and he is still on 55 percent oxygen. They are letting him rest tonight and chose not to try to take him off the ventilator. They may try again tomorrow if they think he is up to it. That's about it for today. Thank you again, everyone, for the continued thoughts and prayers. It means the world to me and my family. —Victoria.

September 17, 2014, 2:45 p.m.

Sorry for the late update today, everyone. My dad is doing well. He did not pass his ventilator test today, but he was still responsive in a positive way when he was off the sedative. He is about to have a bronchoscopy and have some of the fluid taken out of his lungs. His fever is still under control, and there is no sign of infection in his groin where his line was, which was a concern. Still, it's a slow, steady ascent. Keep praying, everyone! —Victoria.

September 17, 2014, 4:17 p.m.

The bronchoscopy went well, but it did show major inflammation in his lungs. They are doing a culture and testing for pneumonia. We should get the results in a few hours.

Another thing I would like to share with everyone is something that I have been discussing with other family members. From this point on, we would like for everyone to respect our wish that only blood family members come back into the ICU and his room. If any close friends would like to come back to see him, we ask that you be escorted by a family member. This shouldn't be a problem because most (if not all) of the time, someone is here who can bring you into his room. The nurses are aware of this wish and will be helping to enforce this rule, but their main priority is my dad's health and taking care of him. If anyone has any questions about this, please do not hesitate to call me or one of my family members. —Victoria.

September 17, 2014, 9:10 p.m.

Tonight was a very short visit. We think it best right now that he let his body rest and be exposed to as few outside germs as possible so that he has time to heal. I made sure to let him know that, as always, we are here for him and that we love him. Tomorrow is a new day, another day for improvement and forward motion. Let's pray extra hard for him tonight. Pray that God continues working in his body and mind and through the nurses and doctors. Let's pray for a peaceful night's rest and that he wakes up even more ready and determined than he already is to kick this sickness once and for all! —Victoria.

September 18, 2014, 1:51 p.m.

There aren't many updates so far today. I spoke to his doctors, and they are just going to continue what they are doing. He's still fighting a fever and the infection in his lung. One of them looks good, but the other looks like pneumonia. He's also back on 90 percent oxygen. This is because he is becoming more easily agitated. His tolerance to his sedative is going up, so it's hard to keep him asleep and fully comfortable. It's possible that they will switch his drug, but the downside is that the other sedatives can take longer to wear off, whereas the propofol he is on now wears off in five minutes or so. This means fewer vent tests and less time to interact with him. But if it means he is comfortable and relaxed, that is all that matters. I will let everyone know if anything changes. —Victoria.

September 18, 2014, 8:56 p.m.

Wow, I can hardly believe a week has already gone by. I can't even decide if it has gone by so incredibly fast or so incredibly slow. I don't have anything new to share about my dad's health right now. He is continuing his current treatment, and the nurses and doctors are still keeping him under close watch and care. These men and women are phenomenal people. They have been so great to keep us informed and keep our spirits up. I also want to speak for my dad and send out a *huge* thank you again to friends and family members who have stepped in to help us in this difficult time without even being asked. I know he is so proud and thankful to have so many wonderful people to call friends. You all are so selfless and true blessings to us. I want to thank everyone for the continued prayers as well, which I know are being heard and are working to help heal him. I guess that is it for tonight. As I mentioned, let's keep those prayers going and keep asking God to do his work in my dad. He is the ultimate healer and he knows how important it is for all of us to have him back in his full health! Until tomorrow. —Victoria.

September 19, 2014, 2:05 p.m.

Hi, everyone. I just wanted to post an update even though there aren't many changes. He is getting another bronchoscopy to rid some of the mucus from his lungs. His doctor is also talking about possibly getting him a special bed. It's called a Rotorest. It works by tilting him from side to side, and this is also supposed to help with his lungs. I did some research on it, and it looks like it does a pretty good job. Thank you all so much, again. Keep praying! —Victoria.

September 19, 2014, 10:26 p.m.

Sorry, everyone, for the late post tonight. I just wanted to let everyone know how my dad is doing; they have him on the

Rotorest bed. I am so excited about this because I have heard so many success stories. They still have him sedated and have been upping the dosage to keep him comfortable. They also have been checking his cultures regularly, and they are all coming back negative. So no pneumonia! As for everything else, we are still the same. Stable, but this is still good. He is improving little by little day by day. Let's keep the prayers going! —Victoria.

September 20, 2014, 12:0 3p.m.

Good morning, everyone; we just finished visiting with my dad and talking with the nurse. There are some major improvements to report. My dad is currently on 75 percent oxygen, and he is saturated at 100 percent. The nurse also said that some of the alveoli in his lungs opened back up. This is a definite step in the right direction. If we can continue lowering the oxygen on the ventilator and he stays saturated, we will have overcome a huge obstacle. And this also could possibly mean his clot is beginning to dissolve. They said his lungs are still inflamed from the bronchoscopies, so they will be letting those take a break. We are moving in the right direction. Keep praying! —Victoria.

September 20, 2014, 5:58 p.m.

Yay! More fantastic news this afternoon: his fever is gone! He's back at 98 degrees and his oxygen is at 50 percent with 98 percent saturation. Things are looking *so* good. They may take him down again tomorrow for another CT scan, so that would help us to know if the clot has gotten any smaller. Thank you, everyone, for praying constantly for my dad. I can't tell you all how much it means to me because I know that your prayers are being heard and answered. Thank you again, everyone; I will post again tonight if there are any changes. —Victoria.

September 21, 2014, 2:39 p.m.

Hey, everybody. Not much has changed since I posted last, so I've waited until later today. My dad has sustained his oxygen levels for twenty-four hours now. He was still at 50 percent on the vent and saturated at 100 percent. The X-ray last night also showed some improvement in his lungs. They are continuing to let him rest and keep healing before doing any CT scans or other tests so as not to agitate him and disturb this positive trend. We will be heading back to the hospital again in about an hour, so I will let everyone know if anything has changed. Thanks so much, everyone! I will keep you all updated. —Victoria.

September 21, 2014, 7:17 p.m.

So there aren't any major changes to report this evening, but he is remaining stable at 40 percent oxygen! We breathe in 21 percent, so he is getting very close to breathing at a normal oxygen level. We just need him to respond in a positive way each time the nurses lower it. Still no temperature and he just looks all around better. Can't wait to see the improvements tomorrow brings. I feel like we are finally on the up and up! Until tomorrow. —Victoria.

September 22, 2014, 12:12 p.m.

Good afternoon, everyone. So we have quite a bit to share. His fever is back. It's probably due to a reaction to a drug they have given him. He has a mild rash, so the fever could be in response to that, according to his nurse. Also his doctor requested consent from his sister to do a tracheotomy. This may seem like a scary thing to be doing, since it is oftentimes considered a "permanent" solution, but I have spoken with two of his nurses and heard from his doctor that they are performing this procedure with his comfort in mind. Normally after ten days, this is a choice families have to make. The tubes in his throat can be very irritating, and they don't want to cause long-term esophageal and lung damage. A tracheotomy also allows them to more easily test his progress and do more frequent vent tests, since they do not have to remove and reinsert his tubes. There are of course some risks involved because they have to take him off blood thinners for twelve hours before they can do the surgery. This puts him at risk for more blood clots forming. And there is also a risk for bleeding once the surgery is done, and they put him back on the blood thinners. The good news is that this is considered a pretty minor surgery, and it is done in his room right at his bedside. We have great faith in my dad and his strength as well because he was at risk for bleeding when they moved his lines from his groin to his neck, and that procedure went beautifully. As for now, we have to wait twelve hours until they do the surgery. Like I said before, he is fighting that fever, but they just gave him a dose of liquid Tylenol. His oxygen levels are still at 40 percent, with his saturation remaining at 95 percent. They also lowered his peep (pressure from the ventilator) from fourteen to eight, which is another improvement. Keep praying, everybody. I will post again if there are any other updates. —Victoria.

September 22, 2014, 9:37 p.m.

Hi, everyone. There are no changes to report since this afternoon. The doctors and nurses are hoping for a very stable night. If he can maintain his oxygen level through the night, they can run more tests. We are still waiting for his surgeons to consult on the tracheotomy with his doctor. I will let you all know when there is an answer. Please, everyone, pray that he maintains his levels tonight. We need a solid night to be able to move forward. Until tomorrow. —Victoria.

September 23, 2014, 1:04 p.m.

Hi, everyone. Last night was a great night! He maintained his oxygen levels, and his fever didn't spike too high. He was at 99.5 when I was there at 1:30 a.m. He's still at 40 percent oxygen, and he's staying saturated at 98 percent. The nurses are going to move him back to a normal bed, so they can change his vent settings to CPAP. This will prepare him for breathing on his own. Hopefully he will respond well. The surgeons are still debating whether or not to move forward with the tracheotomy, and his heart doctor is strongly advocating to not take him off his blood thinners; so we will see how that plays out. I will update when there is more news. Keep praying hard. We're getting there! —Victoria.

September 24, 2014, 5:30 p.m.

I am at a loss for words! They have changed his sedation, and he is *so* responsive. He is answering questions by nodding and shaking his head. He is squeezing hands and moving his arms and legs. His eyes are very open, and he understands what we are saying. I asked him if he remembered getting to the hospital, and he said no; I told him the story about how he got there. Then I said, "Thank God for the girl at your gym who called 911, right?" He shook his head yes. The doctors are thinking of taking the ventilator out tomorrow because he is breathing on his own right now. I am in awe and just praising God at how much he has done for my dad today. We are almost there, everyone! —Victoria.

September 25, 2014, 12:49 p.m.

I would like to share some absolutely amazing news with everyone. My dad is finally off the ventilator and is breathing on his own and sustaining perfectly! We visited this morning, and he was able to talk and carry on short conversations.

He's pretty tired and a little groggy, but we finally have him back. From here on is mostly just rehabilitation and recovery. Praise the Lord for this and how much work he has done for my dad! I am in awe of the miracles he has worked for my dad. The nurses were adamant about keeping visitors at a bare minimum, so we are going to respect that. I know everyone is so excited to see him, but I do agree we should give him a few more days to recoup so that we don't overwhelm him. As soon as he feels up to it, I will let everyone know when they can come and visit. Thank you all so much for praying for him through this ordeal and being so faithful and believing in him. —Victoria.

September 26, 2014, 1:29 p.m.

Hi, everyone. I wanted to give an update on how he is doing today. He's still awake and is able to talk to us and communicate. It's pretty short conversations. But he tells us he loves us, and he lets us know how he's doing. He's such a fighter! We keep telling him that he has to stay strong, and he will be out of here in no time. We're working on getting him to eat, but he doesn't have much of an appetite. He does want a beer though. Ha ha! He's definitely still got his sense of humor. They are giving him some breathing treatments to help his lungs, and as soon as he is able to actually eat, they will start him on oral medications. Progress is progress even if it's only a little at a time! —Victoria.

September 28, 2014, 9:13 p.m.

Hi, everyone. I'm sorry I haven't posted in a while. I'm sitting in my dad's room right now, and the fact that he's been awake and so aware of everything going on has kept me very preoccupied. He has made leaps and bounds in terms of progress, and I'm astonished at how strong my dad is. He's so amazing! Today I came to visit, and he was sitting up in a chair, eating lunch on his own. He has his voice back and is able to form full sentences and have full conversations. The doctors don't have words for what he has accomplished. Neither do I. He wants everyone to know he got through the tough part. He's working hard on getting better for everyone. Isn't that just like my dad? Working hard for everyone else. He is the most selfless man I've ever met. I'm going to post again tomorrow morning and give a more detailed explanation of what the doctors said is going on. But I want everyone to know that he is doing great, and he is so much himself again. I thank God for that. —Victoria.

September 29, 2014, 3:03 p.m.

Good afternoon, everybody. I know last night's entry was kind of vague and didn't give much information, so I wanted to post a few other details today. As of 12:30 p.m. this afternoon, the nurses and doctors taking care of my dad think he may be moved to a different floor. This is a step-down floor and means he is a little bit closer to being able to come home. He no longer needs any form of oxygen assistance, but he is still taking breathing treatments throughout the day. He is more than ready to get up and start getting some muscle strength back, so they have a physical therapist on board; they are working with him to get him moving a little bit each day. They were taking him down for some scans around 1:30 p.m. I think they are checking some of the clots in his arms and lungs. He's finally got an appetite again and is eating and drinking on his own with very little assistance. Memory is looking better than we expected. He is foggy on a few things, but the doctors say that the hypothermic therapy he received can cause some short-term memory problems. This is not permanent though, so he should start to get some of that back over the next few weeks. Overall he is doing fantastic. I know everyone is ready to see him, but I want to wait a little longer. Maybe once he is transferred to the new floor, we can start having a few more visitors. As always, however, please make sure that you are with a family member before going back into the ICU or any of the non-waiting areas. I will update everyone again in a little while. —Victoria.

September 30, 2014, 4:38 p.m.

Hi, everyone. Today has been another great day. My dad was signed off on moving to the cardiovascular care unit. This is considered a step-down transfer, and he is no longer in intensive care. One step closer to being home! He is very comfortable in his new room, and all the nurses already know his name. He's quite the guy over there at Halifax. We are so grateful for the staff members who continue to go above and beyond for him and our family. It was very moving to see the nurses in CVICU saying good-bye to him as he was leaving their floor. As for moving forward, there are physical therapists working with him daily. And from here on they will continue watching the clots in his body and work on getting him on a therapeutic regimen for his medications. Let's get this guy home! —Victoria.

October 3, 2014, 7:56 p.m.

Hi, everyone. I thought I would update tonight, since we have hit another huge milestone. My dad has moved out of the CVCU and into in-patient rehabilitation. He is doing physical and occupational therapy, and his nurses are helping him get used to his new routine. He is getting back into the swing of things. It's hard to believe that one week ago he could barely walk or talk, and now he is sitting up in his bed, eating Chick-fil-A, and watching ESPN. Ha ha! It's a miracle what he has accomplished, and I am so proud of how strong and motivated he is. The nurses expect him to be there until maybe the seventeenth, but he could be discharged sooner. I wouldn't be surprised, since he seems to be on such a fast path to a full recovery. Anyway, I will post again when I have some new information. The posts will probably become less frequent, as I have such little new information to share over the course of a few days. But I promise to let everyone know when anything big happens! Until then. —Victoria.

A message from my dad. October 4, 2014, 8:35 a.m.

Because of you, I am still here. Thousands of e-mails and words of encouragement. But know this, I felt them all! All! Words from all over the world. I love all of you! I'll be out soon. As I sit here in the hospital getting ready for physical therapy, I realize how close I came to death. I saw people who have been gone for a while. My time still may be coming. Don't know. *So many people!* Heaven is perfect.

A Final Update by Victoria Mitchener, December 1, 2014, 12:29 p.m.

Hi, everyone. It has certainly been a while since I posted last, but I wanted to take the time to kind of wrap things up a bit. I can't even begin to explain how it feels to be back on this site. I have to admit that I have been somewhat avoiding reliving the memories of that month my dad was in the hospital. However, it's one of the events in my life—and I'm sure many others' lives—that impact and help define who I am as a person. You can never prepare enough for a loved one to be nearly taken away from you. I never thought I would have to confront a situation like that. But I did, and I never would have been able to get through it without the support from my family, my friends, and my dad's friends. Support from strangers too. It is truly a testimony to who my father is as a person, and I know he is so proud to be surrounded by so many incredible individuals. For that I just want to say thank you. It gave me the strength to get through one of the toughest times of my life so far. There were so many donations, phone calls, cards, visits, and just an absolute outpouring of support from the community. As for the man of the hour, he is doing miraculously well. He's able to drive again, has no life vest on anymore, and his rehab helped him to regain so much of his memory that it's as if he went through nothing at all. He's even allowed to have a glass of wine or a beer occasionally. He is the one who really wanted me to get back on this site and let you all know that he and our entire family appreciate every single one of you. The holidays coming up are times when we surround ourselves with family and friends; sometimes we take for granted what we are so blessed to have. This holiday season I just want to ask that everyone be especially thankful. Take a moment or two to just sit back and look around. Look at your kids, your parents, and your friends; reflect on your health and be thankful that today God has given you the opportunity to be alive. Take that and use it. Never ever take such things for granted. I hope that everyone has a wonderful Christmas and holiday season!

Signing off,
Victoria.

Around 1980 - Eighth grade, giving a speech

Mid to late 1980s - College Days

SOUTH BEND

South Bend
White Sox

MIKE MITCHENER   P

Late 1980s - Professional Baseball

Mid-2000s - Mike's parents and all four children,
Cameron, Connor, Victoria and Sarahbeth
Photo credit: Mike Mitchener

Around 2010 - Mr Cathy and Mike at Sam's Club
Photo credit: Mike Mitchener

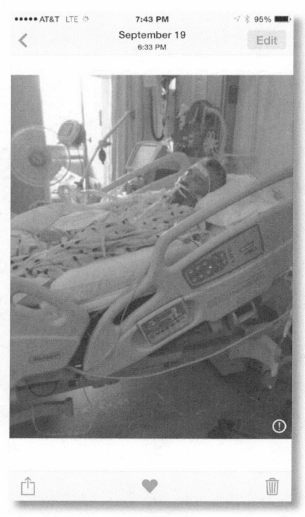

September 19, 2014 Halifax Hospital, the only
photo of Mike taken during his coma.
Photo credit: Dave Davidson

Around 2003 - Mike and Darrell Arnold in Sam's Club
Photo credit: Mike Mitchener

2014 - Mike and Kayli Cantrell

Mike's family 2016
Photo Credit: Mike Mitchener

CHAPTER 17

Heaven Is Perfect

At some point in time while I was in my coma, I found myself standing in a place I had never been before. Above me was a light so bright and powerful that I could barely lift my chin off my chest. I was sure if I looked up into that light I would lose my vision completely. The light felt as though it was right above my head. I could open my eyes, but my vision was limited. I could look down and a little bit from side to side. Looking down, I could plainly see the place where I was standing. I seemed to be on a street of some kind but certainly unlike anything I had ever seen before. This "street" was paved in gold. I saw powerful reflections off the street. On closer examination, I saw that precious stones— like diamonds, rubies, and sapphires—were a part of the streets. The reflections of the powerful light were amazing. My vocabulary cannot provide an appropriate description of this area. It took my breath away. I wanted to know where I was. Was it a dream?

I soon got my answer. I looked side to side, and initially I saw no one. I was alone, or so I thought. This grand place was so beautiful that I felt no fear. Suddenly I realized there was someone standing beside me; he appeared to be someone I recognized. On closer examination, I seemed to be standing next to Truett Cathy. The difference was that Mr. Cathy appeared to me as a younger man. I guessed him to be in his mid-thirties. I looked at Mr. Cathy in this place, and then I looked at myself. He was younger, but I was still the same age as I remembered being. The last time I saw Mr. Cathy before this experience he was in his early nineties. In my vision, however, he was younger, but I somehow recognized him. "Truett?" I asked. He nodded.

What was happening? Where was I? Mr. Cathy simply said, "Let's walk." I nodded my head and away we went. We walked side by side. When he sped up, I did too. When he slowed down, I followed suit. I don't remember much of what he said. But I know I was asking questions, and he was answering me. I was totally mesmerized. Anytime Mr. Cathy had spoken to me in life, I had listened. This time was no exception, for his words always contained passion. He knew when to speak and when to listen. I was glued to him. As the "day" wore on, finally my friend said, "Same time and place tomorrow." I nodded my head, and we parted ways.

The next day we met again, and as with the prior day, the light above my head was incredibly powerful. Once again, I felt as though I couldn't lift my chin off my chest. We proceeded to walk again down the golden streets with the beautiful reflections. They were magnificent. Mr. Cathy spoke with elegance and grace. I was in pure listening mode. I didn't want to miss anything. Like the day before, I stayed right beside him. His words were so pure. I wanted more. Once again, as the "day" came to a close, he simply said, "Same time and place tomorrow." I nodded, and we parted ways. I have no idea where I went on either day when we weren't together. I just knew I wanted to see him again so that he could fill me with joy and knowledge.

Day three came around with a fundamental difference. Either I had become accustomed to the bright light or it simply wasn't as bright. For whatever reason, I could raise my chin slightly. The bright light was certainly still there and so was Mr. Cathy, but this day was different. As I lifted my chin, I saw it. I saw the glory of the place I was in. What captured my attention initially were magnificent buildings. I have seen tall buildings before in New York, Los Angeles, Chicago, and London. All these cities had tall buildings, and in all cases I could look up and see where the buildings stopped. This was different. These buildings went up and up and up. I saw no clouds in the sky, nor did the buildings ever seem to end. I left the street, Mr. Cathy, and my comfort zone. I went over to the buildings, and they too were emblazoned with the same beautiful stones and the same reflections of light. I put my hands out to touch one of the buildings, as they were unlike anything I had ever seen before. I was completely overwhelmed. I moved back to the street where I had left Mr. Cathy. When I asked him about the buildings, he said, "It is where they live."

It was at that moment that I began to realize where I was standing. We continued to walk down the golden streets.

Beautiful buildings on the left were extending as far as the eye could see. Beautiful buildings were also on the right. I was overwhelmed with feelings of peace and tranquility. I was in a perfect place. I was in the most perfect place. I was walking on the streets of heaven. Before this event, I never really tried to imagine heaven, nor did I study about it's appearance. I saw things when I was there that can't be imagined and that are difficult to express with mere words. Every step I took and every feeling I had when I was there was positive and peaceful. When I was there, somehow I was able to experience many emotions at once, and they were all positive. I was filled with joy, comfort, tranquility, safety, and an overwhelming sense of belonging. I was preparing myself to stay in this perfect place forever. Then Mr. Cathy looked at me with his beautiful blue eyes and said, "You must go back." Knowing my journey was complete, I nodded my head without hesitation and simply said, "Okay." Shortly after that conversation, I opened my eyes, and I was in a hospital room.

Sitting beside me was my friend Darrell Arnold. I asked Darrell where I was. Then I asked him what had happened. He proceeded to tell me that I had suffered a major heart attack and that I had been in a coma for fifteen days. I was somewhat overwhelmed with emotion, and I was trying to process everything running through my brain. Darrell told me that the chances of me surviving had been slim, but I had made it. I began to understand what had happened. Things started to fall into place. I felt compelled to tell Darrell about my "dream." I told him that it lasted for three days and that I honestly wasn't sure what I had experienced. As I chronicled it to him in a labored way (I'd just had a breathing tube removed from my throat, and the quality of my voice was quite rough), I noticed that Darrell became very engaged. I told him everything I could remember. When I moved to the part about seeing Truett Cathy, Darrell's face lost all color, and I thought he was going to pass out. With difficulty I asked him if he was okay. Darrell asked me the last thing I remembered, and I said that I remembered going to the race in July. He then asked me what day it was, and I told him it was early July. The actual day was September twenty-sixth. I had lost nearly two months of memory. This type of amnesia I am told is often experienced after such an event. Darrell then informed me that Mr. Cathy had died on September eighth, and I had my heart attack on September eleventh. At that moment I realized my experience was real. My time with Mr. Cathy was life changing. Needless to say, I realized that I had been to heaven. No one can tell me that Mr. Cathy was not in heaven. He was quite possibly the most spiritual man I had ever known, and everyone—including myself—knew that when his life here ended, he would move on to heaven. He was there. So was I. What a gift.

CHAPTER 18

Recovery

After I awoke, the beauty of my family and friends was overwhelming. Obviously I had no idea what had happened, and my memory was not good. I had been told that people from all over the world had come to see me and/or had followed my progress on the web site Victoria had been updating so diligently. Certain people who came to see me while I was in my coma were very affected by my condition. One of those people was Dave Davidson, my first boss's boss and friend of over twenty years from Sam's Club. Dave was sure that I would die and took a photo of me in my hospital bed—the only photograph of my critical illness. What I felt (and it is something I hope all of us feel at some point in our lives) was pure love. I wanted to think that many people were happy that I made it against the odds, but in all honesty, it was I who felt the joy. I felt their love. People kept telling me after I recovered that they were praying for me during this illness. I am compelled to always reply, "I know; I felt all the prayers." I believe that my Father in heaven heard them too. I had come so close to dying, but God decided to send me back. He had plans for me, and I was ready. My experience was real. My passion for the Lord was overwhelming. I had been blessed a long time ago to be able to talk to people. His plan was unfolding.

Physical and cognitive therapy followed. As with my acute hospital care, those folks were magnificent. After the initial assessment, the rehabilitation staff was convinced that I would not be the same. In so many words they told my parents that people with this type of serious event are usually severely compromised if they survive. They were convinced that I might get out of the hospital in six to eight weeks at the earliest. No one bothered to share that information with me. My Father in heaven had other plans. My father here knew that I would battle this like no one else. He had seen it before in his feisty first born and was going to see it again. Thanks, Dad, for instilling this strength in me in an indirect way. People decide their own fates by their decisions, beliefs, and actions. My father taught me that. He never said it; he just lived it and so did his son.

As physical and cognitive therapy began, the outlook for my mental capacity looked bleak. Initial tests indicated that the stroke and multiple heart stoppages might have caused some irreparable damage to my brain. Not good. I was preparing for a fight. Prior to the heart attack, I had never missed a day of work. Had I been sick? Sure, but I had a responsibility to my company and to my family. I was blessed with good health, but there were times I probably shouldn't have gone to work when I did. This stamina was in my DNA.

In essence I was preparing myself for a fight. The fight would be me against this cardiovascular event; four to six weeks of rehabilitation, huh? We'll see about that.

The rehabilitation progressed, and the medical staff was baffled. Here was a guy who shouldn't have lived, and he was flying through their regimen. Two weeks into my rehabilitation, I was told that my physical rehabilitation, as well as my cognitive recovery, was advancing at a pace that was considered almost miraculous. I remember one of the doctors looking at me and just shaking her head. When I asked what was wrong, she simply said, "You're done; you can go home." I remember asking the doctor why she was shaking her head, and all she could say was, "You are a miracle, Mike." I remember glancing up and saying a short prayer. His plan was still unfolding.

The number of visitors who came to see me every day while I was in recovery was staggering. They wanted to see an example of the miracles that God can manifest. People came whom I hadn't seen in twenty-five years. Good people. These people knew I took good care of myself both physically and spiritually. I could see in their eyes the wonderment of a person who survived something that quite frankly he shouldn't have. They wanted to see a miracle, and God put me right in front of them. This was part of God's plan, and I knew it. I didn't preach. I didn't need to. The work of God was clearly apparent. Again, my responsibility to the Lord was unfolding.

I was dismissed from the hospital thirty days after I went in. Not only was my physical rehabilitation fast but my cognitive recovery was a miraculous work of God. My mom reminded me of the ordeal of rehabilitation for cognitive therapy after I left the hospital. They decided that the nearest place was an hour and a half away from home. Since I was not cleared to drive independently, my parents took me to the first session and my dad took me to the rest. Each session was eight hours and my dad drove me from Ormond Beach to Jacksonville and remained there waiting for me to finish and then drove me home. Those were long days. I was still required to wear a defibrillator vest during this time. Since my heart had abruptly gone into a lethal arrhythmia so many times during my illness, they had me wear a special vest for several weeks. This vest had special paddles imbedded in various areas. The paddles monitored my heart rhythm with the purpose of shocking my heart if necessary. It was never necessary. I was soon able to stop wearing the vest. Another milestone.

At one point during the cognitive therapy sessions, there was an emergency and the therapist had to leave our group. She put me in charge, showing me the assignment for the day and left in a hurry. On her return, she couldn't hide her delight when she learned that we had finished the assignments for the day with me as the leader. I found out later that the emergency was manufactured to see if I might be able to lead others again. Mission accomplished. Later on in the sessions, I remember one young therapist asking me some pointed questions about purchasing a car. I was more than happy to help. It wasn't long and they released me from cognitive therapy and some time later, I passed the driving test allowing me to return to work.

I had all my senses back physically, with the exception of some numbness in my left foot. That numbness is still there. I hope it stays for the rest of my life to serve as a reminder of the wonderful things that can happen to a person who believes in God, has wonderful medical care, and has an "I will not lose" attitude. Cognitively, I had one issue that will remain with me forever as a result of the stroke. My short-term memory is compromised. Sometimes I think this was intentional because I now only focus my energies on today and tomorrow. Miracle complete—right? Not quite.

CHAPTER 19

A Calling

The night I was released from the hospital was a beautiful one. It was October 10, 2014, nearly one month after I suffered the heart attack. I celebrated my forty-eighth birthday while still in the hospital. My mom remembers when a friend came to the hospital to help me shave my scruffy face. She was so relieved to see me looking more myself. I was older, a bit thinner, and certainly wiser. I wasn't supposed to live through this situation. I did. I wasn't supposed to be home in a month's time. I was. This was God's plan, and I knew it.

I was very unsettled as I walked around my house for the first time in a month. Mom and Dad had cleaned the house thoroughly. Maybe they had some sort of nervous energy, or maybe it was their way of telling me that everything was going to be okay. I'm not sure, but my house was spotless. On entering, I noticed that my kids were not there. They wanted to give me some space and so all four of my children decided to spend the night with their mom.

My mom took this opportunity to present me with a blank

journal and pen. She told me to write down everything I could remember. She explained that some day I would likely want to review the details of what had happened to me. I had been keeping journals for many years writing to my children and so journaling was familiar to me. But I was still processing what had happened and I couldn't start writing just yet. I put the journal aside, but not for long.

My house was very quiet, and I found myself somewhat restless. After a few minutes, around seven in the evening, I explained to my parents that I was going to go outside and just sit in the back of my pick-up truck. I find comfort in dropping the tailgate, taking a seat, and simply reflecting. I had done this many times before because it gave me a sense of peace. My neighborhood is very quiet, and my street is tucked away in a private setting. There is very little traffic on my street. So off I went to the truck to reflect.

I sat down and noticed something right away. The sky was brilliant with stars. There wasn't a cloud in the sky. The temperature was perfect. I was home and I was alive. I felt compelled to pray. I have a tendency to go into prayer to thank God for the wonderful blessings in my life. This moment was no exception. I realized that the faithfulness and grace of God was present, and I felt that it was time to pray. It was just me, a soda, and a beautiful night. Sitting on the tailgate of my truck, I sat my drink down, bowed my head, closed my eyes, and went into prayer.

What do you say when you finally have a chance to reflect and tell God your thoughts? My mind raced, and I searched for the right words to say. Honestly, all I could muster were two words: *thank you.* I realized that what I had been part of was special. Was I supposed to feel bad that a healthy man of forty-seven years had suffered a major heart attack, coupled with other significant medical issues? Was I supposed to worry about what to do now that my life had been turned upside down? Again? I don't really know what I was "supposed" to feel, but what I felt was gratitude. The only thing I could say in my prayer was thank you. That's right. I was grateful for being chosen to see heaven and the glory it represents. That's all I had. Just thank you. Once I opened my eyes, I realized I wasn't alone. Standing in front of me were two people. They were clothed in exactly the same way—white tunics, gold sashes, and sandals—but there were unique differences. The man to my right was about seventy-five years old. He had gray hair, a gray beard, and brown eyes that were locked on to me. The man standing beside him on his right had a brown beard and brown hair that flowed beautifully. He was about thirty years old. He also had the same brown eyes. I knew that these two were one and the same. It was the Father and Son. It was God and Jesus Christ. They had a message for me.

I took a deep breath after composing myself. Looking at each one of them, I asked a simple but pressing question: "Why me, and what now?" These two men, in perfect harmony, looked at each other and then looked at me. They took a deep breath and said two words: *Be patient.* They spoke in perfect harmony in voices that sounded like nothing I had ever heard before. After giving me this message, they turned and walked away. Another miracle.

I was not overwhelmed. I was not in an emotional state. I

had a clear and pure purpose. All of it made sense now. I was the one who had been chosen to see this vision. I was being prepared to share my experience with others. God didn't want me to bow in reverence. He manifested in a way that invited me to not look away. He wanted me to see his direction, and I did. God and his Son had a message for me. They delivered their message, and it was now time to respond. I got off the tailgate, grabbed my drink, and closed the tailgate. Maybe I was closing the door on my old life. I'm not sure, but I certainly felt that I had a new responsibility. It was time.

Old life is over. New life begins. Seems somewhat like a conclusion. By the time my experience in the back of my truck happened, I had resigned myself to the fact that I was to be a spokesperson for the Lord. I had no formal training, but I did have a few special gifts. I had the gift of faith. I wasn't a pastor, but I believed in God before my heart attack; now my faith was simply and purely strengthened. I also was given that rare privilege of seeing heaven with a man whom I considered to be one of the strongest Christians I had ever known. He was there, waiting for us to join him. You may ask, who is *us? Us* represents the people of faith. They are the people who cling to the knowledge that God is real. Jesus Christ is real. Heaven is real. I am one of those people. I saw it. I was supposed to die. I didn't because of God's plan for me and his faith in me. I was convinced that I had a responsibility, a big job. I have never backed down before, and I won't back down now. Let's do this.

I received a phone call soon after I got out of the hospital. As a matter of fact, I received several phone calls, but this one was different from the word go. On the other end of the phone was a good friend who explained to me that her sister was dying, and she was scared. I had never met this person. However, I felt compelled to help. I asked my friend to have her sister call me so that we could talk about death, faith, and life. Heavy stuff, but it was time to start telling my story. It was time to start telling God's story. I realize that both God and Jesus Christ told me to be patient, but I was also moved to talk to this person who was not sure about what was going to happen.

Two days later, my phone rang. The formalities didn't take long, and the realization that this person was scared hit early in the conversation. She had battled cancer for several years, to the amazement of the doctors. However, the end was near, and she knew it. She and her husband spoke to me for fifty-seven minutes. It is important to note that my time on the phone rarely lasts longer than five minutes. I'm just not a phone person. This was different. We spoke about experiences. We spoke about faith. She had confided to me that she was a good Christian, but death was imminent, and she was scared. She didn't know what was coming next. I did. As the conversation wound down, I realized something glorious. She was no longer scared. I explained to her that if she believed in God, she was getting ready to enter the most perfect place. I had no idea why God selected me to both experience heaven and to be able to come back and talk about it. The unknown can be scary, and it can play tricks on your mind. Regardless of how strong your belief is, sometimes you become scared when death is imminent. She was scared. Her husband was scared. I told her that when she got to heaven, she would no longer be in any pain. She would walk the beautiful streets as I had done. There would be sadness in the people she left behind on earth. I realized that this too is a function of faith. Sadness comes to those who lose loved ones. Her husband would be sad. He would be challenged with faith issues. "Why did this have to happen to me?" It's normal. We are not designed to fully understand God's plan. We simply aren't. I didn't understand what happened to me, but I did understand my role in the lives of others. About two months after we spoke, she died. Now she waits. She waits for her loved ones who believe. However, when they are reunited in heaven, they will be together in perfection forever—never to be separated again. Perfection waits for those who believe.

Some time after those calls and a few other in person testimonies, I found that journal my mom had given me and I started writing. Getting started was the hardest part. But once I started to describe my experience it became easier and easier. I would write pages and pages and then feel physically exhausted requiring rest to recover. Even though I struggled with the words to describe the events and the details, I never once struggled to remember what happened when I was in heaven or the beauty and wonder and emotions of that experience. Initially, I was just trying to document my memories for myself. It wasn't until later that someone suggest I fill in more details and write a book. I was slowly being shown that my purpose was beyond just talking with one person at a time.

I ask myself daily why I had this experience. I was a believer. I lived a good life. I prayed daily, but I was far from perfect or even overly religious. Why me? Why was I the one given this wonderful opportunity to glimpse heaven? I honestly still don't have answers for all my questions. That's God's plan. He is the Creator. He saw fit to allow me to experience this near-fatal event, to see heaven, to recover, and by the following spring to walk my daughter down the aisle as she married the love of her life. Another miracle. What a privilege. Why me? I don't know.

One thing I know for sure is that if you believe in God, you are guaranteed a place in perfection. I firmly believe that place is really indescribable in words that we can comprehend. Heaven is perfect. It is the reward for a person who believes. We all make mistakes. I believe that those mistakes will not keep us out of heaven, provided we have an unwavering belief in God. Our time on earth is so very fleeting. It is over in a minute relative to eternity. Our lives in heaven have no end dates. We walk the streets forever. We are guaranteed joy. I want to go back when God is ready for me to return.

This story is directed to those people who know God and believe. I know there are those who don't believe in anything; if my story inspires them to learn more, I am grateful. I don't presume to know how one strengthens faith in God, but I hope my story provides reassurance and comfort. I can't explain how or why this happened to me. The Bible tells us that God can use anyone, and I'm happy to deliver his message to anyone who will listen. But it's more than a message about believing. It's a message about God's faithfulness in us and his willingness to be with us even during our darkest days. I saw the glory of heaven. By the grace of God, I saw it. I hope you see it too.

Epilogue

Music has been important to me my whole life. Like many people, I can hear a song on the radio and my mind goes back to the past; to where I was when I first heard it. Some moments are forever linked to the music playing at that time. Likewise, my worship experience is enhanced by music each week and like many, I am drawn to Christian music in particular. Since my illness and recovery, I have been drawn to Mercy Me's song "Bring the Rain". It moves me like no other Christian or secular music even years later. The lyrics especially describe the experiences of my life. I have had my share of sorrows but more importantly, I have been blessed with great joys. Read the lyrics of the song for yourself and remember that through the rain, comes great joy. I wish you all the chance to praise God without ceasing even through the rain.

Bring the Rain - Songwriters: Billy Montana and Helen Darling

> *"I can count a million times*
> *People asking me how I can praise you*
> *With all that I've gone through*
> *The question just amazes me*
> *Can circumstances possibly*
> *Change who I forever am in you*

Maybe since my life was changed
Long before these rainy days
It's never really ever crossed my mind
To turn my back on you O Lord
My only shelter from the storm
But instead I draw closer through these times
So I pray
Bring me joy. bring me peace
Bring the chance to be free.
Bring me anything that brings you glory
And I know there'll be days
When this life brings me pain
But if that's what it takes to praise you
Jesus, bring the rain
I am yours regardless of
The clouds that may loom above
Because you are much greater than my pain
You who made a way for me
By suffering your destiny
So tell me, what's a little rain
So I pray
Bring me joy, bring me peace
Bring the chance to be free
Bring me anything that brings you glory
And I know there'll be days when this life brings me pain
But if that's what it takes to praise you
Jesus, bring the rain"

—Recorded by Mercy Me

About the Author

Author Mike Mitchener
Photo by Argyle Photography, Greg Hunter

Mike Mitchener is the father of four children: Victoria, Connor, Cameron, and Sarahbeth. When asked what he does for a living, he simply states, "I'm a father." Whether talking about his professional baseball career, twenty-five years working for the same company, or family, Mike always seems to answer with simple yet complete answers. Mike currently resides in Ormond Beach, Florida.